PIERO   NATHALIE

SARTOGO GRENON

PIERO NATHALIE
SARTOGO GRENON

ARCHITECTURE IN PERSPECTIVE

FOREWORD BY RICHARD MEIER

THE MONACELLI PRESS

First published in the United States of America in 1998 by
The Monacelli Press, Inc.
10 East 92nd Street, New York, New York 10128.

Library of Congress Cataloging-in-Publication Data
Piero Sartogo and Nathalie Grenon : architecture in
perspective / foreword by Richard Meier.
p.   cm.
Includes bibliographical references.
ISBN 1-885254-51-2
1. Piero Sartogo Architetti Associati.
2. Architectural practice, International.
NA1123.P518P54   1997
720'.92'2—dc21   97-5768

Printed and bound in Singapore

EDITOR: RICHARD L. WENTWORTH

COVER: NATHALIE GRENON

DESIGN BY DOMITILLA SARTOGO

Contents

Dedicated to Roberto Burle Marx, architect, sculptor, artist, friend, who made landscaping into a fine art.

Foreword
Richard Meier

As an architect, I believe that what we do is part of a continuum. Architecture is related both to history and to the present moment. It is the result of an inner dialogue, a conscious creative effort to give form to space, the space we move through, exist in, and experience. Architectural ideas address the structure of space, the scale and ordering of space, the flexibility or the rigidity of the organization of space, the relationship between interior and exterior space, the character and demarcation of space, the transformation of space, the materialization (or dematerialization) of space, the poetry of space. Architecture is the thoughtful making of space. The critical force of the work of Piero Sartogo and Nathalie Grenon is its capacity to deal with serious and substantial architectural issues, clearly expressed in form and space.

In 1972, I was in Rome looking at architecture and saw, among other things, a wonderful exhibition entitled "Vitalità del Negativo" at the Palazzo delle Esposizioni on the Via Nazionale, which Piero Sartogo had curated. The exhibition, which had an extraordinary catalog, addressed the emerging change in architectural sensibilities in Italy. This change, realized by the younger Italian architects, was synthesized in the exhibition into a very polemical and powerful statement.

Later, during the period when I was resident architect at the American Academy in Rome in 1974, Piero and I had time to share thoughts, experiences, and musings about the culture of architecture. Piero was at that time just completing the design and installation for another enormous exhibition: "Contemporanea," which was to be located in a parking garage below the Villa Borghese Gardens. In addition to discovering and transforming the most unlikely place anyone could think of for an exhibition of art, this hypersensitivity to the cutting edge was clearly an indication of things to come. Even the plan of the exhibition was on the one hand futuristic and on the other hand spatial, allowing all the arts — architecture, photography, performance art, concrete art — both to coexist and to have a life of their own.

This shared moment of exploration and human perception in the arts and architecture was the beginning of a long friendship. My stay at the academy was enriched by the sojourns and the experiences that Piero made possible.

Like all young architects, Piero struggled through these early years, actively involved in the ongoing architectural discourse. Manfredo Tafuri has put in vivid perspective the importance, especially since the end of World War II, of such Italian architects and planners as Albini, Figini and Pollini, Gardella, Libera, Quaroni, Michelucci, Moretti, Ridolfi, Rogers, and Scarpa. Their influence stemmed not only from the quality of their work but from their position as "father figures" for the generation of younger architects, who were faced with an architectural culture marked by historical richness. Piero responded to this challenge with a realism based on an understanding of the forces consolidating the world through communications and an awareness of the importance of identity in a period of rapid and continuing change.

His work assumed quality as its objective, and historical, topological, and morphological analysis as its method. Certain constants emerge, having to do with context, with the concept of place, with modification or transformation, with the relationship between the intervention and its surrounding condition. It was only in the early 1980s, however, that Piero realized many of the ideas that had been expressed in his previous projects. The project for his Fashion Institute of Technology, displayed in mock-ups at the Urban Center in 1983, gave physical evidence to the realization of many of his heretofore unbuilt works. Equally dynamic and important in Manhattan was the showroom for Bulgari — a jewel of a showroom — on Fifth Avenue and 57th Street. Later his designs for the Italian Trade Center and the Banca di Roma were also noteworthy contributions to the fabric of New York.

This accretion of ideas, this accretion of ferment (which existed for the individual building as well as for the urban scale), has come together again, at the Italian Embassy currently under construction in Washington, D.C. This building certainly marks the integration of both the European and American perspectives of Piero and Nathalie's work. I should note here that the architecture, design, and urban plans of Piero's early career reached fruition not only in the architecture of the Italian Embassy but also at a point when he had been joined by Grenon.

Even in the early exhibitions, there is a concern with the expression of structure, a concern with tactile quality of materials, that finds even richer expression in the mature work. This approach is exemplified in the Italian Embassy by the tectonic use of stone, rarely seen these days in this country, a search for an expression of materiality in which surface and volume find richness.

As European architects with a world perspective, Nathalie Grenon and Piero Sartogo have a body of work that is about ideas — ideas on the making of space, ideas on the materiality of surface, ideas on the relationship of built form to urban fabric — and clearly have an understanding of the specifics of each situation, which enables them to offer an important contribution and a clear message to the culture of architecture.

Introduction
Piero Sartogo

One fall day in 1971 the telephone rang. It was Professor Bruno Zevi and he was shouting at me. "Sartogo, how can you construct a building a few yards from my house without letting me know? I'm calling you from a public phone on the sidewalk near the project. You've got to come here at once!"

Zevi, for me, was a legendary figure in Italian architecture. Until then I knew him only from his writings and from a few lectures I attended at the University of Rome.

The telephone call seemed important — it even worried me. So I immediately went by motorcycle to Via Giovanni Battista De Rossi where the new building for the Rome Medical Association was just peeking out from its scaffolding. A few minutes later, I found myself standing on the sidewalk next to an animated, gesticulating figure wearing a large bow tie. I found the great critic stopping passersby, grabbing them by the arm, pointing up to the building, and asking them, "Isn't it beautiful? Isn't it beautiful?" This scene repeated itself several times as I stood by, a somewhat dumbfounded spectator.

At a certain point, Zevi turned to me and hugged me, saying, "Let's go onto the site. I want to see everything." We crawled in and out of spaces all over the building, from the foundation to the roof, walking up and down the stairs several times, frequently consulting blueprints and models of the project. He was explosively enthusiastic, embarrassingly so for me. Finally he bid me goodbye, saying, "We've got to tell the people about this immediately!"

Piero Sartogo (left) with Walter Gropius, founder of the Bauhaus, at the Architects Collaborative in Cambridge, Massachusetts, in 1964.

And off he went to write a powerful article for L'Espresso, an influential Italian newsweekly, in which he praised the organic quality of the building, comparing it to a tree with exposed roots and using it as ammunition in the battle against the rationalist and postmodern tendencies in architecture. In his opinion, the building represented "a nonconventional list of functions, free from overwhelming syntactical expressions; a language that, by cutting out vernacular idioms and preconceived contextual historicism, falls into the mainstream of the modern movement in Europe."

My encounter with Zevi was not my first encounter with a critic. When I went to Cornell as a visiting professor in the fall of 1969, I brought with me the ideological influences of the left-wing student movement in Europe. So not surprisingly, I expounded to the students, in my very first meeting with them, my passion for avant-garde and anticonformist ideas, such as the integration of technology into architecture.

I was particularly taken at that time with the work of Archigram, Cedric Price's British countercultural architectural group, which proposed a series of avant-garde concepts, such as the Walking City (constructed on telescopic legs) and the Plug-In City (consisting of units that could be discarded when obsolete). All its creations were movable, flexible, adjustable, and so on; all were conceived as megastructures containing the city. One work, by Yona Friedman, was just a space frame suspended in the air. A microcosm of this theoretical approach had just been realized in the campus of the Free University of Berlin, designed by George Candilis.

The students seemed to be in a state of shock throughout the lecture, simultaneously fascinated by and afraid of my radical departure from the school's accepted doctrine.

The next morning I was walking through the campus green. Suddenly I saw a man, readily identifiable from his idiosyncratic dress as English, standing in the middle of the lawn and pointing at me with his walking stick. The stranger could only be Colin Rowe, the university's architectural theorist, though how he recognized me I'll never know. Evidently the students had reported my lecture to him.

"Piero, Piero, you are wrong," he shouted across the campus. "Architecture in which everything moves, in which everything is interchangeable, undefined, flexible, is not architecture. You're not talking about architecture, but only science fiction for Hollywood."

I followed him to his house, where he bombarded me until late in the evening with one book or manuscript after another. Everywhere I looked in the house, in fact, there was nothing but books and manuscripts. The house itself seemed like one giant book.

"You come from Rome where you have everything. Look at it carefully. The lesson of

From left to right, critic Bruno Zevi, Piero Sartogo, Fiat chairman Gianni Agnelli, Senate President Francesco Cossiga, and two union representatives examine a project for the reuse of the Lingotto factory in Turin in 1983.

At Cornell University in 1969, Piero Sartogo explains some of his heretical ideas to Colin Rowe, theorist of the school of architecture.

architecture is all there and I will show it to you. Why are you wasting your time with this other stuff?"

As he continued his harangue against my theories, he went from Piranesi's visions of Rome to the Nolli plan and beyond, showing me that what was needed was urban space and the proper structuring of that space. He impressed upon me that the city is made up of public voids, such as piazzas, gallerias, porticoes, streets, etc., carved out of the solid mass of the urban fabric. As a Roman, I knew these things, but I had never before read them as he was.

Being stubborn by nature, I persisted in imparting to my students my original ideas by day. By night, I visited Rowe, who tore my ideas to shreds and set my thinking to work along new lines. Apparently not new enough, however, because I have never been invited back to Cornell.

The lesson from this experience, which has stayed with me to this day, is that the intellectual labor of architecture comes before any three-dimensional elaboration, and that a building is an organizational system (the archetype), which becomes architecture only when it is altered and distorted by setting it into a context, both physical and cultural.

As every architect knows, the archetype is the three-dimensional interpretation of the functional organization of a building. The archetype of the Renaissance palazzo is always the same, and yet the architectural configuration is realized in a variety of ways. The archetype follows a precise functional and spatial formula. The ground floor, with its atrium and grand staircase, acts as the transition between the public street and the private inner court of the building, around which are large enclosures for carriages and the adjacent stables, granaries and storehouses, guards' rooms, and the like. The second floor, the so-called piano nobile, is where receptions take place; it is therefore a sequence of large salons, galleries, and loggias, all with very high ceilings. The floor, or floors, above is used for the apartments of the owner and the owner's family. The floor immediately underneath the roof, due to its barely livable heights and climatic conditions, is traditionally used for servants' quarters.

It is easy to identify the functions of the floors from the facade of a Renaissance palazzo, due to the heights of the floors and the dimensions of the fenestration, among other things. From this layout emerges the enormous scale of the front door leading into the atrium galleria. Although what I have just described is the standard archetype, each palazzo has an architectural configuration that is different from any other in order to respond to their different contexts. Some are free-

Studio in the Rome apartment of futurist painter Giacomo Balla.

standing cubes (Palazzo Strozzi in Florence), some are pentagonal (Palazzo Farnese in Caprarola), some are trapezoidal (Palazzo Borghese in Rome), and so on.

The Renaissance palazzo is part of my historical background. Because I am Italian, I was and am immersed in an environment characterized by centuries of architectural tradition. From this dense stratification of artifacts, I have always wanted to extrapolate whatever I could find that expressed modernity. The Italian futurist movement — with the urban visions of Antonio Sant'Elia, Mario Chiattone, and Virgilio Marchi — became my point of reference. So one day in the early 1970s I paid a visit to the Rome apartment of Giacomo Balla, the only leading futurist still alive.

If Rowe's house was like a book, Balla's house was like a painting. I felt as though I was entering a world of signs and colors that covered everything (from the floors to the walls and doors to the ceilings to the windows to the furniture), modifying the physical shapes and dimensions of all the elements into a new space determined by perception.

At a one point, Balla pulled out his famous 1913 project for the Lowenstein House in Dusseldorf, his first move toward the abstract representation of speed, light, and movement. What stood out was his process. On a standard perspective of a dining room with table and chairs he had superimposed a visual structure of signs and colors running over and incorporating everything (even a painting on the wall) in such a way that the original perspective existed and did not exist at the same time.

Looking at this piece of art, I saw at once the fantastic possibility of designing architecture not only as space but also as a system of visual performances. Designing the space and visual performances together would transform the space-time sequence of the physical entity, as in the painting.

At that time I was working on a public-housing development in the Milan hinterland adjacent to Sesto San Giovanni, historically the center of the working class. After a crude but realistic analysis of the situation (the building program, the planning regulations involved, the chaotic context of factories, buildings, and illegal housing), I decided to organize the site with a system of repetitive towers grouped in threes, setting them on the flat land and leaving the greatest possible free space among them.

I then introduced an inclined plane that intersects all the towers; the surfaces below the plane are white and those above are black. The resulting segmented line of separation produced a volumetric articulation reinforced by the two colors. From a distance, the towers seem to be a townscape of scattered elements. From the park of the new development, the scattered towers appear to be a united mass, which disintegrates into fragmented surfaces when viewed from the pedestrian paths.

The volumetric configuration was the point of departure for the design, as the perspective of the dining room was the point of departure for the Balla painting. The juxtaposition of the perceptual structure on the volumetric elements modified them into a new space determined by perception, as in the Balla painting.

My theoretical assumption was that architecture is a transmitter of images and that these images vary according to the point

Ceiling designed by Giacomo Balla for his house.

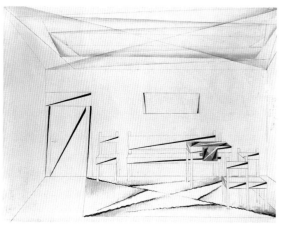
Project for the dining room of the Lowenstein House in Dusseldorf by Giacomo Balla, 1913.

from which they are observed; thus, the visual performances of a building can be designed to respond to the modes of perception deriving from its context. The result is a very strong conceptual link between construction, site, building, urban fabric, and territory.

In short, a certain desired image can be formed only in a specific place. With this strategy, different places at a distance from each other can be visually connected, becoming part of a perceptual sequence and therefore part of a spatial continuum.

On the basis of my past experience (the Gescal Public Housing Development in Milan, the Rome Apartment, the Bergamo city district master plan, etc.), it was only natural that I should come to know the author of Visual Thinking. I met Rudolf Arnheim in his lonely hermitage on Lake Erie in the summer of 1979, after a long exchange of letters based on photographs and drawings of my past works and those in progress. Arnheim wrote the essay "Living Space in Counterpoint" in the early 1980s, which is being published in this book for the first time.

In the meantime, Nathalie Grenon and I began to practice together, combining her pragmatic intuition (partly due to her multicultural upbringing) with my Italian humanistic culture. After studying urban design and architecture at the most avant-garde schools in America and Europe, Nathalie arrived in Rome. With a grant from the Italian government, she did postgraduate research at the UNESCO ICCROM Institute, which specializes in historical preservation and restoration.

From the beginning, Nathalie's work was very successful. For example, our first collaboration was "Italian Re-Evolution: Design in Italian Society in the Eighties"; she was cocurator, designer of the installation, director of research, and editor of the catalog. In the process of compiling the exhibit, Nathalie traveled all over Italy for more than a year, seeking out striking examples of everyday items from coffeepots to Borsalino hats to piazza pavings to scooters, some conceived by the most famous Italian designers, others by figures who remain anonymous to this day.

Her meticulous research included photographing street signs from Bolzano to Palermo. The words were the same — Via Roma, Corso d'Italia, streets that exist in every small village — but each of the more than one thousand renderings (which she included in a sequence in the exhibition) was completely different in terms of graphic characters and materials. The sequences showed the diversity and versatility of Italian designers, even

Piero Sartogo and Nathalie Grenon at work in their studio in downtown Rome.

those living and working only a few miles from each other. Nathalie clearly demonstrated that Italy, in a century of standardization, refuses to conform.

It should be no surprise that "Italian Re-Evolution" received great critical acclaim as it traveled throughout North America in the early 1980s. The catalog, filled with contributions from the best-known personalities in Italy's cultural and artistic circles — Umberto Eco, Giulio Carlo Argan, Gianfranco Ferré, Giancarlo Menotti, Gianni Bulgari, Sergio Pininfarina, and so on — received international recognition, including a best-publication award from the American Association of Modern Art Museums in Chicago.

If I were to compare our work to the game of chess, I would say that I move linearly, like the pawns, bishops, and rooks, while Nathalie moves randomly and unpredictably, like the knight. This dual strategy offers a better chance of winning the game. In our work as architects, Nathalie and I combine our fortes to address the possibilities of conceptual space — the dimension beyond reality, the surreal possibility that lives within the physical structure of rooms and buildings and that needs to be articulated.

The manipulation of form by designers and architects has a long and rich history. In our practice, we have concluded that there are two sides to experiencing forms: one is the acceptance of literal reality, the other is the manipulation of people's perception of that reality, so that it becomes something new and different. This we call "virtual architecture," and it is predicated more on perception than on function.

When a designer accepts the idea of this split, it opens up an incredible potential — one that has always been there, by the way. In Italian Renaissance or baroque design, the city was perceived as a theater, a stage for the masses, a collective imaginative creation. But somehow, starting roughly at the beginning of this century, architecture lost that interest: buildings were conceived as self-contained replaceable objects, with little or no relationship to the contexts within which they were placed.

Nathalie and I believe that architecture should be something much more than a series of independent creations. The architect has an obligation to give coherence to something larger than a building's mere physical existence. It does not serve people's needs to design buildings that can be placed here or there or anywhere, no matter how beautiful they may be. There is always, in any given spot on earth, an assertive element that should be responded to — the path of changing sunlight, the topography of a hill. There are always elements within the environment — other buildings, natural vistas — that offer a proscenium for viewing the construction.

The Parthenon is a classic example. Because the Greeks wanted to view the temple, set on an Athens hilltop, as a true parallelogram, they could not build it with four straight sides. They had to introduce a series of distortions —

for example, the slight slope of the columns — to counterbalance the normal optical illusions that viewers experience at a distance. The Greeks, by doing this, presented the appearance, if not the fact, of pure form.

The Greeks worked with the perceptual viewpoint of the pedestrian in mind. Today, however, the concept of mobility has been totally revolutionized. With the introduction of airplanes and automobiles, we no longer get around principally on foot.

And yet, though today's designs must deal with the effect of being viewed at different speeds and heights than centuries ago, the problem is identical: to create something that is both context-sensitive and need-serving, rather than replaceable and interchangeable. We contend that the image — the qualitative scenario — produced by the design of a building or urban space should be responsive to the way that this building or urban space is viewed. And the designer has the potential to control this response by specifically programming the viewing experience.

The designers of the older cities of the world were sensitive to this potential, and in many situations they realized it magnificently. They understood the importance of the spaces between and around buildings (what we call "urban voids"), and they shaped these spaces in unique ways.

Think of how Michelangelo designed the Piazza del Campidoglio in Rome. He repeated the angle already set between the Palazzo dei Conservatori and the Palazzo del Senatore by building a symmetrical palazzo — it had no set purpose — at the same angle on the opposite side of the Palazzo del Senatore. Accepting this angle as a point of departure, he set about to treat the space it created. The decision he made is remarkable: the angle between the two flanking buildings of the Campidoglio and their relationship in perspective (as diminishing or increasing apparent distances), in conjunction with the oval form of the star-shaped paving pattern as well as its three-dimensional projection on the subtly designed steps that surround it, gives the square a totally stereometric monumental appearance.

Think, too, of the gallery designed by Filippo Borromini in Rome's Palazzo Spada, where the diameter, height, and spacing of the columns change incrementally, forming a built perspective. The result is that the apparent length of the gallery dramatically increases or diminishes in relation to the position of the viewer.

Nathalie and I purposely design each project twice. The first effort is very cool, rational, based on utilitarian needs — where the supporting walls are, how many people must be accommodated, how high the ceilings should be, and so on. Then, designing on top of that first plan, we start to define the visual potential within these limitations, such as the movement patterns and the prominent points of view.

The first project interprets the functional program volumetrically, the second interprets the of the place with signs that define the perceptive performances sought in those specific time-space conditions. The combination of the two plans, actually visible on overlapping transparent drawings, gradually determines the architectural configuration and its language.

We purposely tend toward complexity of forms. A single answer cannot serve. An environment has to be supportive of its occupants' constant day-to-day psychological changes. A visually complex project gives them more options for experimentation. We believe that the ideas of contamination, ambiguity, and differentiated levels of participation are vital forces in design.

We find, perhaps surprisingly to some, that our clients have no difficulty in responding to these complexities. Whether consciously or unconsciously, people are desperately looking for an urban environment with which they can identify. We feel that there is an enormous unrealized potential for the creative manipulation of space, both in the urban design and in the architecture of cities.

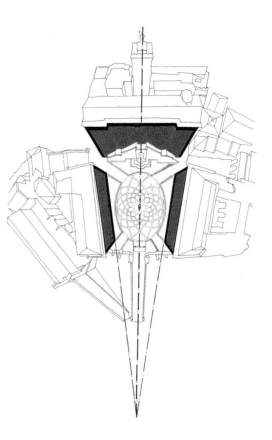

Michelangelo's Piazza del Campidoglio in Rome, showing the perspective layout of the square.

As Le Corbusier says, architecture lives in the solitary, persistent, "patient research" that is later seen in the works themselves. In this long and tiring journey, the voices that come from within are those of the artist and the people with whom he or she comes in contact, whereas the voices from without are those that give the work its sense of history.

Precisely in order to listen to the latter voices, which taken together mirror our identity, Nathalie and I have put together this book, which juxtaposes architectural criticism with the praxis of the project and its construction. It has been deliberately designed to go from the present backward, searching out the roots of what we do while at the same time looking forward.

Palazzo on the Potomac

Italian Embassy, Washington, D.C.

2

It's December 1996, and you're driving over Rock Creek Park on the Mass-achusetts Avenue hill. The construction trucks and cranes are gone at last from the wooded site at the end of the bridge. Peeking through the leafless treetops in glorious winter light is this curious, um, Italian country house? Quickly, you make a left onto quiet Whitehaven Street N.W.: You have to see this thing. The reaction would please architects Piero Sartogo and Nathalie Grenon. "The building," they said last week after the design for a new Italian Embassy was unveiled here, "is the memory of a palazzo." A memory filtered through dreams of centuries of stone villas in the Tuscan hills, of Renais-sance courtyards framing the sky in harmonious proportion — "Man did this!" say the strong wooden eaves — of Alberti, Michelangelo, and anony-mous craftsmen, of Roman prototypes, of Plato's pure forms.

1. Model of new Italian Embassy in Washington, D.C., from Rock Creek Park side.
2. The embassy model as seen from Glover Bridge, leading toward the Massachusetts Avenue hill.
3. (overleaf). The cut through the middle of the embassy opens views from Whitehaven Street to Rock Creek Park.

BENJAMIN FORGEY
The Washington Post
December 18, 1993

Of course, one cannot with certainty predict how well a building finally will work and look by examining preliminary models and sketches and floor plans. But neither can one easily resist the poetic reach of this particular project. It isn't hard to understand how a competition jury selected it from a group of nine designs invited from a virtual Who's Who of contemporary Italian architects: Aldo Rossi, Piero Sartogo, Renzo Piano, Vittorio Gregotti, Vico Magistretti, Guido Canella, Gae Aulenti, Carlo Aymonino, and Vittorio De Feo.

All the competitors were asked "to make a building that would somehow be Italian," Sartogo and Grenon recall, and they were told to make it compatible with its surroundings. It is from these two vaguely conflicting requirements that the Rome-based architects began to work out their brilliant, multileveled metaphorical design.

They felt compelled to become intimately familiar with the site, flying here to see it firsthand. It's big: about five acres of woodland bordering Rock Creek Park. It's totally unlike manicured Italian countryside: raw North American hardwood forest. Sartogo took the trouble to observe that it's on the dividing line between Washington's dense center and the suburblike patterns of upper Northwest. And, as have many architects before (but none of the other Italian contestants), he became fascinated with Washington's geometry, noting that the site is on one of the many odd-angled intersections dictated by L'Enfant's plan for the city. Sartogo the pedagogue pronounces, "Architecture begins when the prototype is distorted by the site." (He's taught in Rome and at Cornell and other American universities). The site-induced distortions of his prototype — the Italian villa — begin with the basic floor plan. The four-story building is square, like the original 100-mile plot of Washington (before the Virginia part was receded to the state), and it's split diagonally with a pathway through the middle, or almost the middle, just as the Potomac River divided the Washington square.

Though the building is by necessity set back quite a distance from Massachusetts Avenue, the architect wanted to make a symbolic gesture toward it, as it is the "public" street in comparison to residential Whitehaven. Sartogo/Grenon simply aligned one side of the square parallel to the avenue, and that side became the main ceremonial façade. Such "distortions" in plan and elevation continue: Unlike the other

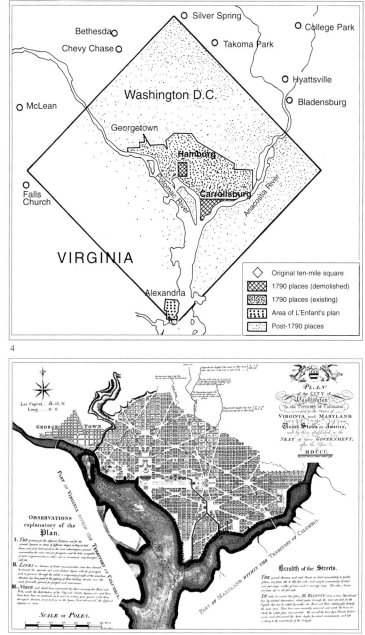

4

5

4–5. In January 1791, by decree of George Washington, an area in the form of a perfect square, 10 miles on each side, was chosen on the eastern branch of the Potomac River to become the new Federal City (fig. 4). The area, located centrally in respect to the 13 original states, is now known as Washington, D.C. In June 1791, Pierre Charles L'Enfant designed the grand scheme for the Federal City (fig. 5), a baroque plan characterized by a wide central mall and 13 grand avenues radiating outward from the center, one dedicated to each of the original 13 states. Massachusetts Avenue, one of these 13 grand avenues, stretches from the center of the city westward to an area typified by rolling hills and woods. The buildings lining the avenue define its particular spatial, dimensional, and architectural character.

Italian Embassy, Washington

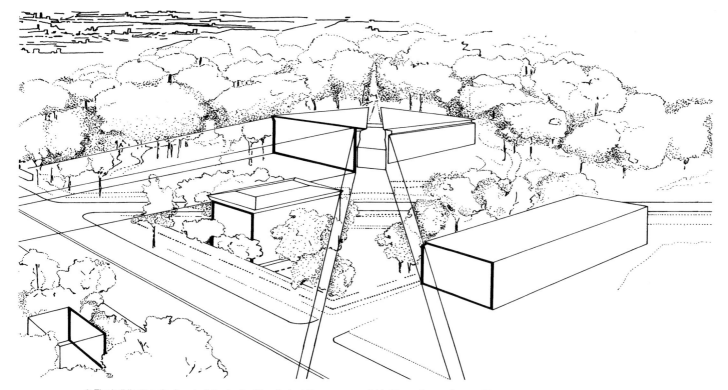

6. The building's major façade, following traditional orientations, runs parallel to Massachusetts Avenue. The cubic volume opens along one of its diagonals. This opening, running north to south, not only preserves but strengthens the connection between Whitehaven Street and Rock Creek Park by effectively forming a gateway to the project and site. The gateway is also visible from Massachusetts Avenue.

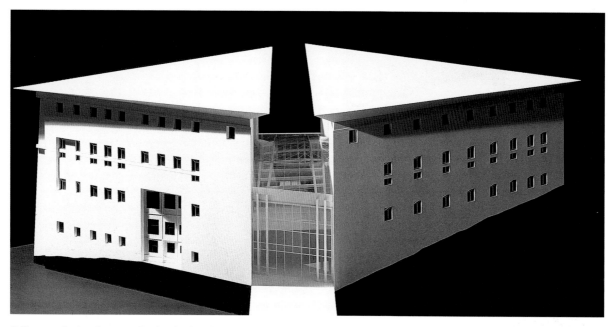

7. The carved-out portion, a two-level pedestrian circulation system, is in fact a broad path that runs through and beyond the entire structure, opening it up boldly.

three façades, which are conventionally straight up and down, that bordering the escarpment down to Rock Creek is angled outward, mimicking the steep slope. It's like a buttress, holding up the castle on the hill.

And yet for all of these supple accommodations to its specific site, the design remains powerfully Italian in a dreamlike, cubical way. The cut through the middle has a surreal decisiveness about it. So does the wonderful roof, a vast, slightly canted copper cap atop the sliced cube. Nothing is quite normal, quite perfect.

The roof has strong, cantilevered eaves that recall those of Renaissance palazzi and also emphasize that the roof is not quite centered above the square. It is as if this big thing had somehow been pushed askew, like all mortarboards at all commencement ceremonies.

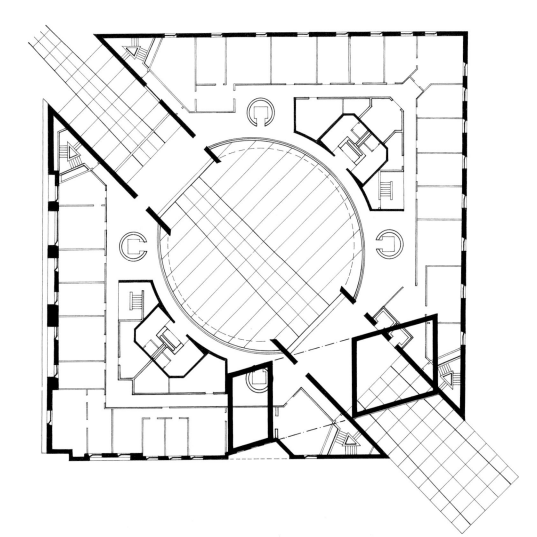

8

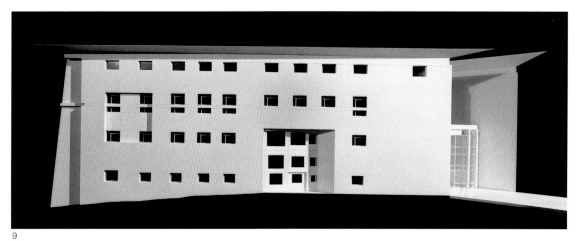

9

8–9. The cubic volume that opens along one of its diagonals establishes an asymmetrical composition (fig. 8) in which the entry door appears to be in the center of the building but is asymmetrical in the façade facing Massachusetts Avenue (fig. 9).

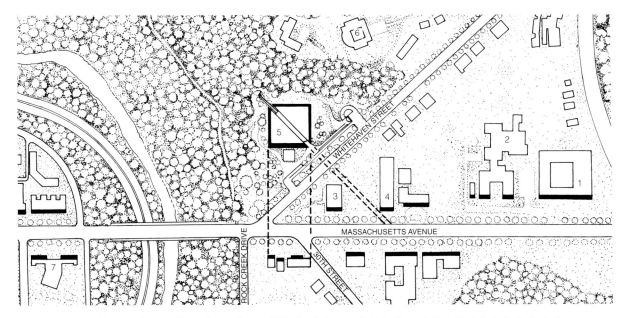

10. Located along Whitehaven Street at Massachusetts Avenue, N.W., the site is a wooded lot adjacent to Rock Creek Park. Distinctive in its appearance west of 16th Street, Massachusetts Avenue boasts some of the city's finest examples of residential architecture, variously designed in the Beaux-Arts and Classical Revival traditions. These stately edifices, many of which are now devoted to foreign mission use, derive their character from a shared respect for uniform height, rhythmic placement, consistent setback, and alignment with the avenue. 1. British chancery. 2. British residence. 3. Brazilian residence. 4. Brazil chancery. 5. New Italian Embassy. 6. Center for Hellenic Studies. 7. Islamic Center.

Likewise, the VIP door in the main façade is a huge dark void, shielding a giant gate of copper with differently sized rectangular glass openings — it's a cathedral door in a little monastery. The door is off-center, and thus confounds Renaissance symmetry. But if one allows one's eye to "complete" the square, where the walls would meet had they not been sliced well, one realizes that (of course) the door is precisely in the center.

Such architectural games would be mere conceits were they not firmly grounded in a clear, strong concept. The design is slightly wrong, but it's all right. It's powerful, yes, but it's also quite modest. The architect obviously took to heart the request that it be compatible with the nearby mansions, although Ambassador Boris Biancheri deserves credit, too. He made sure that immediate neighbors and all nearby Advisory Neighborhood Commissions were alerted well in advance. In fact, neighborhood concerns about parking, tree removal, and noise were written into the competition guidelines by Leo A. Daly, the Washington architecture firm that is assisting on the project.

One thing that Sartogo did besides burying the parking structure as required was to burrow the building into the sloping ground. Consequently, the northwest façade, closest to the neighbors, is only three stories high. He also made sure the embassy didn't have the look of an office building plopped down on neighborhood ground. To discourage the office look, the guidelines stated that only 35 percent of exterior wall surfaces could be glass. The percentage in these walls is much less, though I suspect the reasons are as much aesthetic as they are contextual: Sartogo's "villa" is decidedly introverted.

But it's welcoming, too. That's the function of the big cut through the cube. A passerby can see right through the building. The architect even provided a platform off the Whitehaven Street sidewalk to encourage people to enjoy the view, and he made it even more dramatic with a paving pattern that exaggerates the perception of receding space. At the opposite end will be a fetching little overlook from which to take in a spectacular vista of the park and the Washington Monument.

Inside, as in any self-respecting palazzo, there's a central courtyard — circular, in this case. This is, of course, the principal gathering place. All of the most public functions — auditorium, cafeteria, library — are accessible from it. But it's difficult at this point to visualize the interior spaces, even this big central one, for much remains to be worked. The architect speaks, for instance, of a lens-like glass structure that will have the effect of a transparent dome rather than a simple skylight. And he's being forced to consider a bridge linking the third-floor offices across the big slice.

So, we'll wait and see, but with great expectations. As I said, it's hard not to be enticed and even (a little) entranced by Sartogo's succinct vision, this strange stone-and-copper villa high in the forest.

11. The linear geometry of the path crossing the building intersects the cylindrical volume of the lobby. The transparent dome is therefore conceived statically as a system of load-bearing arching girders, which support the transverse center-bits. The longitudinal girders envelop the whole structure, marking with pilasters the two fronts: one looking on Whitehaven, the other on the park.

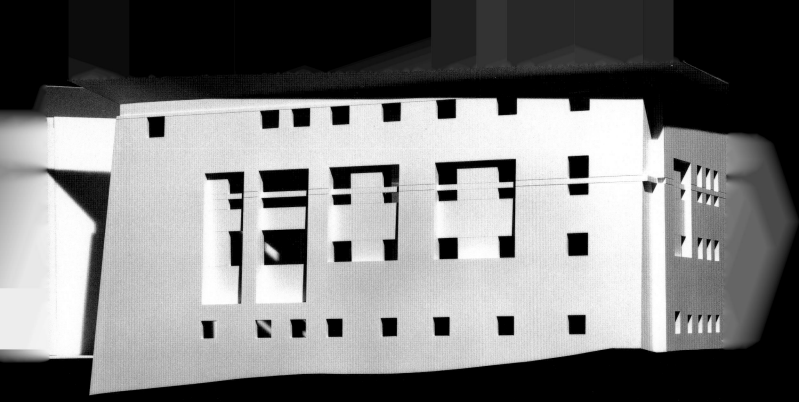

12

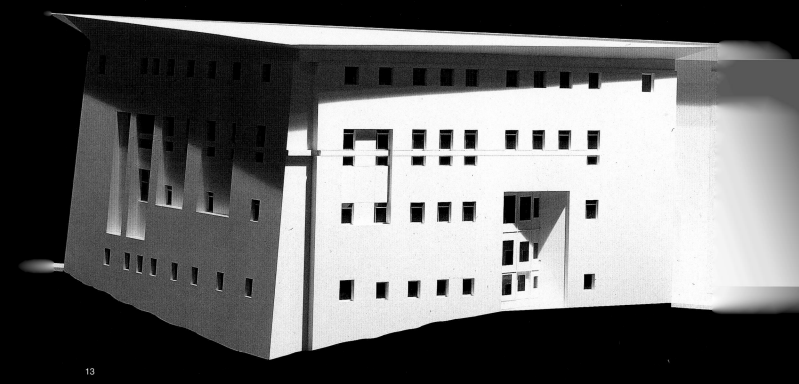

13

12–13. In the façade facing Rock Creek, nearly immersed in the woods, the building's mass counters the steeply sloping land with the incorporation of a buttress (fig.12). The major façade and the buttress create a node whereby the meeting of the two planes, vertical and inclined, is clearly demonstrated. Indications of the floor-slab levels and of the vertical planes of the fenestration emerge from these geometries as connecting elements in the

Manhattan Headquarters

Banca di Roma Building, New York

2

In mid-Manhattan, on a street between Madison and Park Avenues, the transformation of the urban fabric from residential to commercial use was almost radical, because of the repetitive gigantism of the International Style of the '50s and '60s.

MASSIMO DI FORTI
Il Messaggero
October 31, 1994

As a result the streets, as we see them today, are, unlike the avenues, very narrow in proportion to the height of the buildings and resemble "canyons" carved out of the solid mass of edifices. Thus we view the building façades only from very oblique angles, resulting in a marked distortion of the perspective.

The fact that a small open quadrangle existed opposite the site of the Banca di Roma Building enabled the architects to counter the matrix of oblique perception with that of frontal perception. The result is nothing less than a compositional tour de force that recalls Borromini's Oratory of St. Philip Neri in Rome as it was originally conceived, before the demolition took place to open up Corso Vittorio Emanuele. Borromini could never have envisaged its present setting. In fact, he had purposely designed the façade with calculated concave and convex surfaces because it faced onto a very narrow street that excluded a frontal view. This particular spatial situation, emphasizing the oblique perception, magnifies the myriad of volumetric articulations of Borromini's façade, illuminated by angled, never frontal, light.

Today the houses in front of the building are no longer there. The street has become a kind of square, and the façade, as a result of the frontal light, seems absolutely flat, though this is not the case. One has only to draw near and stand at its foot to sense the extraordinary quality of Borromini's design. As a Roman, Sartogo is so fully aware of these issues that he has made them the basis for his project on 51st Street.

The system of solids and voids, the lime plaster walling, and the fenestration of the façade follow two simultaneous patterns of perspective increments: The sections of wall widen as they descend toward the ground, and the openings do the same as they progress toward the top. This mechanism of perspective not only shapes the solution of the top and base, but also establishes the relationship between the frame and the central volume, expressed by the recessed surface and the concave copper ribbing. These latter produce a concave effect on the central part of the façade when viewed from the foot of the building. The central recess and the frame are essential to the unity of the overall composition, which is strengthened by the monochromatic use of materials such as white Venetian stone and stucco. The constantly changing dimensions in the solids versus voids tend to eliminate any traditional dimensional values. The building presents itself as an abstract form of powerful impact within its contextual environment.

The apparently extraneous look of this building represents a challenge to the commonplace and repetitive gigantism of the curtain wall, so popular in the years of the International Style. This style was introverted and out of context with its surroundings. The new structure underlines the importance of reestablishing the scale and relationship between building and street. Complexity of architectural matrices, uniformity in volumetric height, and continuity of façade surfaces all contribute to the design of the street. This building should set a precedent for these concepts to be applied.

1. Banca di Roma Building on the south side of 51st Street, Manhattan.
2. Filippo Borromini's Oratory of St. Philip Neri in Rome.

3. Copper ribbing converging toward the center reinforces the façade's concave effect.

4

5

4–5. The two-story atrium of the bank building projects itself on the street as a stone monolith (fig. 5). When the bank is open, the monolith becomes penetrable (fig. 4).

6. The façade follows two simultaneous patterns of perspective increments. The sections of the wall widen as they descend toward the ground and the fenestration does the same as it progresses toward the top.

7. A stairway connects the two executive floors of the bank building. This foyer leads to the boardroom.

8. At night the progression of perspective is marked by beams of light on the edges of the building.

Acropolis in Taiwan

City Civic Center, Taichung, Taiwan

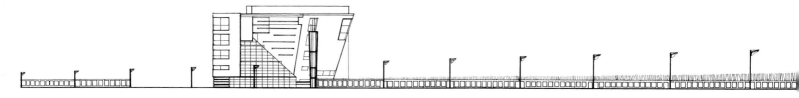

The jury (Yoshinobu Ashihara, Japan; Max Baecher, Germany; Arthur Erickson, USA/Canada; Romaldo Giurgola, USA/Australia; Pao Teh Han, Taiwan; Kiyonori Kikutake, Japan; Joshua Jih Pan, Taiwan) of the International Competition for the new Taichung City Civic Center gave the project of architects Piero Sartogo and Nathalie Grenon (together with Afra and Tobia Scarpa) the only honorable mention awarded.

RICHARD REID
Unpublished article
1995

The art of town-planning can be defined as the ordering of spaces by means of buildings. The nature of urban space and place bears direct and reciprocal relation to the building, giving it definition, and to the life of people within the space, the public "voids" of the urban fabric. Space ordered by buildings may take on a residual aspect or may acquire its own integrity and life, confirming its positive spatial and vital presence in the city. There are numerous precedents in the historical repertory that have served for centuries as referential models for urban design: from the Renaissance square in Pienza, which organizes the Town Hall, Palazzo Piccolomini, and the cathedral into a unified entity, to Alvar Aalto's contemporary Village Hall at Säynatsälo, which resembles a modern acropolis in the woods around its square.

Within the planned development of the Taichung City Civic Center district in Taiwan, the organization of the open space is the primary functional element as a system of access to either the buildings or the park. Its definition as urban space is achieved in the proposed master plan by introducing an architectural promenade that takes on the form of a street with a sequence of "voids" bounded by structures: The buildings and the street form a spatial "continuum" underlining their relationship with the natural open space of the park, providing a dynamic interplay between the carefully unified configuration of the City Government–City Council complex and the entropic edges of the surroundings. It is a city space primarily devoted to pedestrian mobility, but flexible enough to be opened up to vehicles for parades, festivals, and institutional events at any given time.

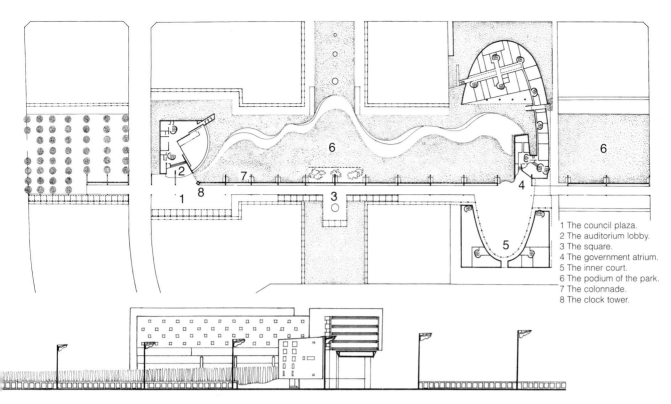

1 The council plaza.
2 The auditorium lobby.
3 The square.
4 The government atrium.
5 The inner court.
6 The podium of the park.
7 The colonnade.
8 The clock tower.

1. Plan and longitudinal section of new Taichung City Civic Center project in Taiwan: The visual effect is to shorten the apparent length of the promenade between the council plaza (far left) and the inner court of the government building (right).

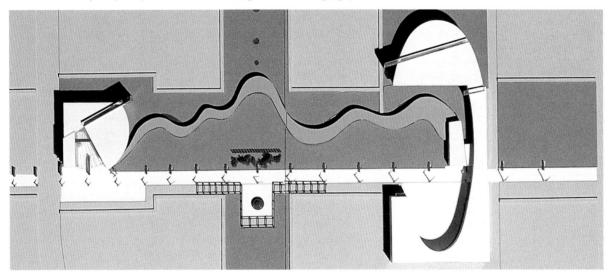

2. The master-plan model.
3. The two sections of the city administration become one unit through the design strategy of the geometric matrix.

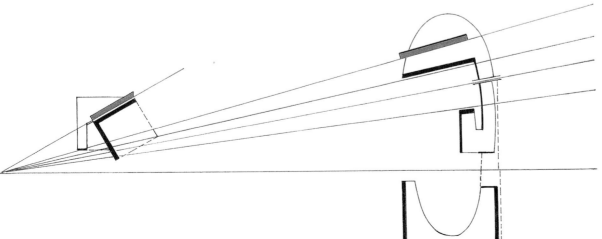

3

4. The promenade from the City Council.

The structured space of the promenade is the regulating matrix of the composition and contributes to the clear and unified image of the new Civic Center.

It is a street having a defined volume of an urban nature rather than being a collection of ad hoc, picturesque, or artificial fragments. It is marked at the points of access by porticoes and screens inserted in a colonnade that projects a rhythm along its entire length. The bays are further defined by seating areas, steps, and plaza openings forming the podium of the park. The clock tower at the end of the arcade system, which indicates an opening to the council plaza, and the atrium and court of the City Government building represent the two opposing focal points.

From the City Council, the flagpoles are positioned in a progression of changing intervals and heights. The effect is to shorten the apparent length of the long promenade from the main entrance of the City Council. This is achieved by distorting the normal perspective perception of the receding space, since theoretically the intervals at which the places recede from the eye will be progressively countered by a growing increase in the intervals between the subdividing planes and by an equally compensating increase in the height of the flag standards and size of the flags. This is a conscious reversal of the scenographic format of Renaissance space, which reached its apotheosis in Michelangelo's Campidoglio, where two lateral palaces were designed and built in perspective to give the viewer the image of an apparently stereometric volume.

The clock tower marks the progression along the promenade and helps to direct people toward the sloping glass enclosure of the City Council multistory lobby. This structure is the spatial pivot of the sequence of architectural frames, screens, and nodes, but its design also alludes to the symbolic status of "township." Within the context of the future development of the urban fabric, the government-park-council complex is the predominant landmark in the area, both for its size and its unity. The uniform height of the buildings chosen by the architects is an element that counters the longitudinal configuration of the site.

The choice of a reduced scale for the articulation of the functions and volumes toward the inner space contributes in blending the natural setting of the park with the scale of the buildings, giving the park a very strong identity.

The elliptical shape of the City Government building, which adjoins the promenade along the park, projects the life of the

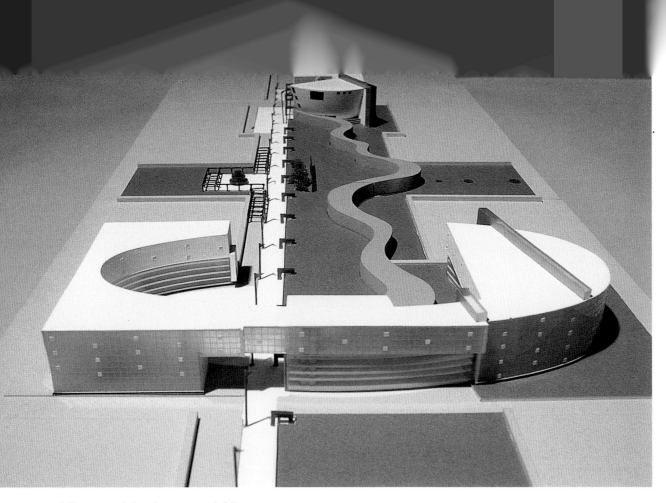

5. The promenade from the government building.

building into an inner controllable pedestrian urban space. As in an arena, the focus is toward the *parterre* in the center, and the views toward the outside are contained within the elliptical skyline: This configuration gives an inherent sense of totality and participation to anyone on the *parterre*. A five-story entry portal marks the transition along the promenade from outer to inner space: At this specific point, we have the main atrium and the mayor's offices, housed in a freestanding palazzo overlooking the park, government, and council, positioned face-to-face to underline their close liaison. As with most renowned institutional complexes, the inner court is a ceremonial place of entry. The spatial relationship established is the determining factor for the specific design of the City Council building: The base cube parallel to Shin Jien Road has been carved out and a portion of it rotated to house the principal public functions, such as the assembly hall, auditorium, cafeteria, restaurant, and library. The vectorial alignments are inserted in the form of emerging skylighted galleries, which interact with the same elements of the City Government building. The geometric matrix indicates the strategy to achieve unity between the two sections of the Civic Center.

The use of smaller structures on the principal axis, the hierarchy of proportions and rhythms in the sequence of buildings, the rotation of hills and flat ground, of open and closed areas between buildings, are all elements that reveal a dynamic conception of space and compel the observer continually to move his point of view. Along the sequence of real and virtual views, each element is distinct from the other but linked together by the subtle harmonies and perspective axes on which the whole composition hinges: a way of conceiving things according to Chinese garden aesthetics, which calls for a succession of even, contrasting impressions and a sequence of European scenographic features that continually involve the observer in an accumulation of images and impressions. And so the two visions of space and world are balanced; the Chinese paratactical one of sequence and the European syntactical one of perspective.

This concept has a well-known precedent in China, which inspired the 18th-century Emperor Yuan Ming Yuow in the design of his Summer Palace park and garden outside Beijing.

The Ultimate Winery for Chianti

Badia a Coltibuono Winery, Tuscany, Italy

1

PAOLO CORBINI
L'Unità
April 14, 1996

Looking at the model, one's first impression is that of a museum, an arts-and-crafts center, or a research establishment. But located in the heart of Chianti, the project logically turns out to be a new winery. Building in the countryside and not in an urban area is difficult, but when the location is Chianti, which lies between Siena and Florence, and when the project is industrial typology for Badia a Coltibuono, a producer of worldwide renown, it becomes even more of a challenge.

Sartogo-Grenon have carried out this project in a small valley sloping down from the little village of Monti toward the Arbia River among vineyards, olive groves, and wooded hills. The result is a project that contextualizes the high-tech industrial typology with the *genius loci* through a powerful architectural composition that interprets the extraordinary qualities of the site, extrapolating its ecological values.

"Chianti," says Nathalie Grenon, "is like a Japanese garden — small, dense, and entirely man-made; a natural yet artificial setting whose equilibrium is founded on a multitude of meticulously articulated geometrical patterns, as in a Paul Klee painting, and on the architectonic repertoire that has been stratified over the centuries. It is an environment distinguished by the harmonious values of a rural culture and by a scale in which man is the measure, all miraculously uncontaminated by the brutal aggression of industrial prefabricated shells."

The winning stroke has been the functional disarticulation of the volumetric elements that characterize the various phases of the process, from the harvesting and pressing of the grapes to the fermentation and aging of the wine. The decision to erect the largest building of the complex at the foot of a wooded hill makes it possible to set up a process of winemaking based on descent by force of gravity, in line with the most advanced winemaking theories, and to obtain a "protected" interior space with very significant ecological energy-saving characteristics: Since the vines are planted according to the position of the sun and the type of soil, the architecture has been carefully inserted into the landscape to obtain natural ventilation and the specific interior thermal conditions necessary for the process.

1. The Badia a Coltibuono Winery is in Monti di Sotto, Italy, at the foot of the wooded hill sloping into the valley of rows of grapevines and olive groves in front of the village at left in model.

2. The design mechanism leads to the introduction of a cylindrical corner solution and an elliptical volume, which contains the main vertical path.

The configuration is that of a bastion, a buttress of terrain with ramps, stairs, passages, and terracing both inside and out that mark various itineraries, not only necessary for the winemaking process itself but also to accommodate the numerous visitors who gather during harvest time. The system of ramps, stairs, and terracing gives structure to the space-time sequence of the itinerary accompanying the winemaking process: Starting out from the belvedere in the woods where the grapes arrive, it runs down the side of the hill, continues across the sloping-roof terracing of the fermentation vats and storage rooms, enters one of the volumes, exiting onto a staircase in the corner of the building that divides and heads in two different directions — toward the cellar entrance on the one side or to the tunnel for the aging of the wine on the other.

3. The powerful unifying element of the design is the transverse linear skylight, which breaks up the stereometry of the building blocks.

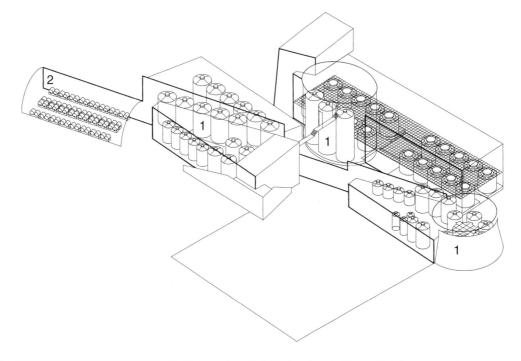

4. The process of winemaking is based on descent by force of gravity. 1. The three large buildings, with their numerous wine vats, are centers for fermentation. 2. The arch-shaped underground structure is the wine-aging cellar.

5–10. Views of winery under construction.

The powerful unifying element of the design is the transversal linear skylight that breaks up the stereometry of the building blocks. The resulting three-dimensional elements are interpreted as brick monoliths by using a continuous facing that envelops both the wall and sloping-roof covering. The deconstructivist design mechanism also leads to the introduction of a cylindrical corner solution and an elliptical volume that envelop the main vertical path. There are two perspective patterns: the first expressed in the above-mentioned volumes, whose joints in the stucco facing widen as they descend toward the ground; the other in the buttress wall fenestration, whose spacing widens as it progresses to the two extreme corners. The dynamic vector introduced by this mechanism is a morphological characteristic that can be found in ancient works of military engineering and one that Francesco Di Giorgio experimented with on several occasions. It has been adopted in civic constructions in the Siena region and has been used in this project to stress the volumetric disarticulation and compress the size of the complex by relating its scale to that of the village of Monti.

Without resorting to the vernacular and using a plain modern idiom even in the employment of materials (brick, zinc, glass, plaster), this project adheres to the very best tradition of organic architecture, which blends the built form into the topography of the land, determining a continuum between constructed space and natural space.

11. The configuration is that of a buttress of terrain with ramps, stairs, passages, and terracing both inside and out. The three-dimensional elements are interpreted as brick monoliths by using a continuous facing envelope both for the wall and for the sloping roof covering.

Chianti Winery, Tuscany

To Siena With Genius

Master Plan of District between Station and City Center, Siena, Italy

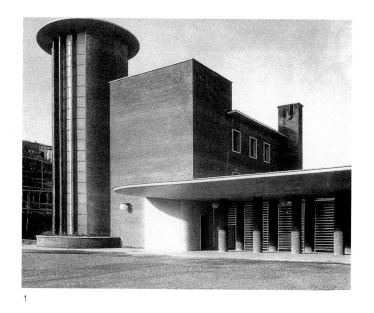

1

BRUNO ZEVI
L'Espresso
August 1, 1996 The world's most important landscape architect, Roberto Burle Marx — at the invitation of Piero Sartogo — participated in "From the Station to the City," a competition to redesign the train station district between two streets, De Bosis and Vittorio Emanuele Boulevard, in Siena. The main thrust of this project, according Sartogo, should contain elements of urban development — such as "urban voids," squares, arcades, streets, subtracted from the solid mass of the urban fabric — to reveal the continuity of Sienese identity. With this, the other determinant elements of identity are the farm valleys and fields that project up to the walls and into the city itself.

The project, developed with Nathalie Grenon and Fabrizio Mezzedimi, contains a system of functional units linking the railway and bus services through underground moving walkways with an elevator that follows a slope and takes passengers upward to three levels. The first is in a linear building, containing a hotel, shops, cinemas, and offices. The second elevator is to the newly designed park. The third and final takes passengers to Siena's historic center.

In this way, the buildings and infrastructures are infused with the dynamic forces of the city. Though Burle Marx died June 9, 1996, Siena will retain the imprint of his genius, along with that of city planners Luigi Piccinato and Piero Bottoni.

1. The original train station in Siena, as designed by Angelo Mazzoni, with its Tower of Light.

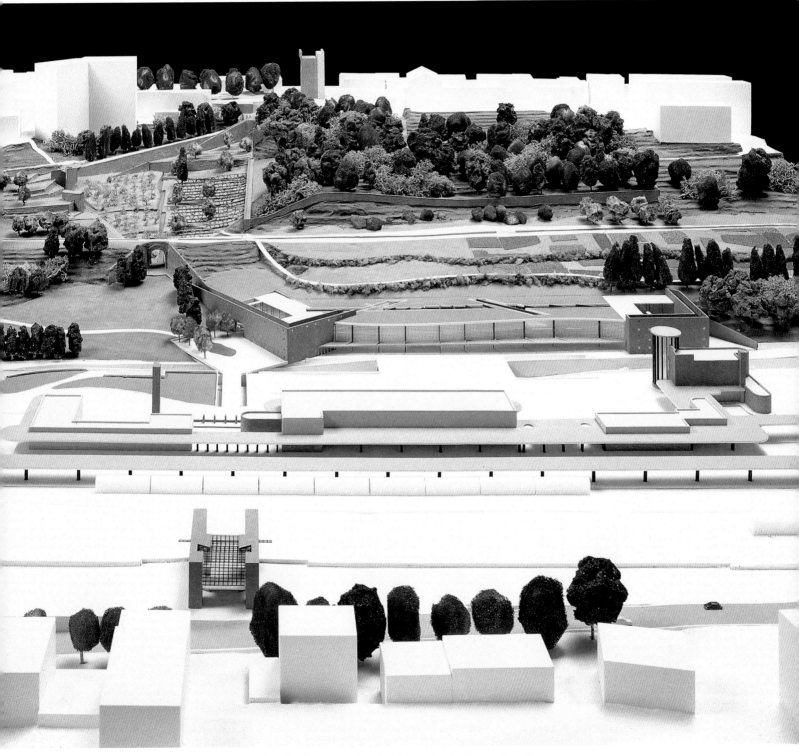

2. Master-plan model of the Siena city district from the railway station to the historical center: view from Via de Bosis.

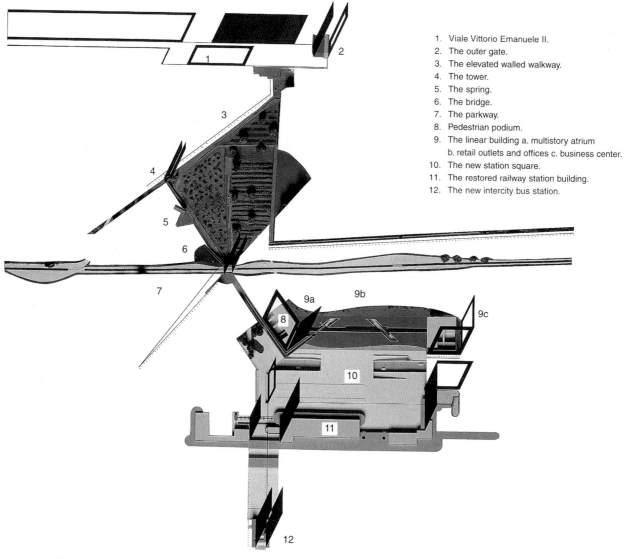

1. Viale Vittorio Emanuele II.
2. The outer gate.
3. The elevated walled walkway.
4. The tower.
5. The spring.
6. The bridge.
7. The parkway.
8. Pedestrian podium.
9. The linear building a. multistory atrium
   b. retail outlets and offices c. business center.
10. The new station square.
11. The restored railway station building.
12. The new intercity bus station.

3. Design concept.

The railway station in the valley is centrally located in the area of intervention and is the most prominent existing modern structure to which the project makes reference. The building designed by futurist architect Mazzoni in 1934 was reconstructed in the 1940s following bomb damage to part of the edifice during the war. Much of Mazzoni's original architecture disappeared in the reconstruction. One of the municipality's competition objectives was the idea of reinstating the original form of this modern Italian masterpiece.

Interpreting what we might call the genetic elements defining the true identity of Mazzoni's original design, the winning solution, by Piero Sartogo and his colleagues Fabrizio Mezzedimi, Nathalie Grenon, and landscaper Roberto Burle Marx, has projected its spatial dynamics in such a way as to involve the whole area from the valley up to one of the main gates of the city.

Siena today, within its medieval walls, is almost totally pedestrian, due to the gradual development of a "park and drive" system with small parking lots positioned outside the walls within easy access of the various city gates. Within the network of transport systems in the valleys around the old town, the northeast side of the city has a concentrated pole of interchange (trains, buses, cars) at the railway station.

The objective was to solve the problem of today's congestion and provide a coherent infrastructure between this pole and the old town for intercity buses, trains, and cars as well as pedestrians.

4. At the top are Viale Vittorio Emanuele II and the outer gate. Underneath is the valley basin. The parkway runs above the park. The new station square dominates the lower portion with the linear building facing it above. Below the railway tracks is the new intercity bus station.

a

c

b

d

VIALE VITTORIO EMANUELE The tree-lined street running from the Camollia Gate to the massive arched structure of the Outer Gate is the northeast arrival point of the mechanized linear pedestrian link from the valley and the main walkway of the park. The first emerges on the side of the street where public transportation facilities run straight to the center (fig. a). The second drops dramatically into the valley in the form of a steep flight of steps at the foot of the Outer Gate (fig. b). In this area, the master plan foresees an extensive development of university facilities on the site of the former Lamarmora army compound, the transformation of Piazza d'Armi into an urban park, and the construction of underground parking lots below Piazza Amendola and Piazza V. Bersaglieri.

e

THE WALKWAY SYSTEM The walkway system is made up of two distinct segments: the upper elevated section heading toward the Outer Gate and the lower one directed toward the railway station atrium, following the slope of the terrain, going under the bridge, and terminating in the south block of the linear building. The elevated section overlooking the valley has the configuration of a buttress wall (fig. c) positioned in the former site of the ancient fortifications built between 1552 and 1555, designed to protect the space between the Camollia Gate and the Outer Gate. Like a medieval city wall, one can walk along the top (fig. d) and descend flights of steps built into a running parallel to the wall structure (fig. e) to the lower level of the park.

i

THE PARKWAY

Partially elevated and partially built into the hill-side during the first half of the 19th century, the parkway is like a promenade along a flat surface. It was formerly the bed for the tracks of one of Italy's first railway routes between Empoli and Siena. The promenade offers an exceptionally panoramic view of the city stretched out along the old Via Francigena, at the same time dominating the valley where the railway station is located, with the hills of Chianti in the background. The parkway links up two densely populated residential areas. On the side of the hill it has a curvilinear edge and blends itself into the natural contours of the landscape. Running down the center is a cycle track, which as a historical reminder, reproduces the route taken by the old Leopold I railway.

j

THE VALLEY BASIN

The natural basin conceived as a conservatory of rural culture is characterized by linear terraced vines intermingled with supporting fruit trees (fig. f). This is a system that has survived to this day as a result of the former allocation of allotments, orchards, and olive groves, which have molded the physiognomy of the Sienese landscape. A stream in the center (fig. g) runs down as far as the bridge, goes underground, and reappears in the form of a fountain in front of the linear building.

j

k

THE SPRING AND THE TOWER

The existing spring (left) has been redesigned and integrated with the new structure of the tower (right) containing the elevators and stairs. Together they form a recreational and rest area along the path of the walkway system.

THE BRIDGE

The bridge is a large brick single-arch structure built at the time of the construction of the railway network. From the walkway positioned diagonally below it going uphill, it forms the gateway to the valley basin (fig. j). Going downhill instead it represents the transition point between the serene atmos-

5

5–7. The organism of the railway station was designed in 1934 by Angelo Mazzoni with a linear front facing the railway tracks and an enveloping shape embracing the square in front. Two large open porticos on both sides of the atrium projected the view of the passing trains into the square outside; likewise, arriving passengers could see the square from the tracks. Transparency, light, and dynamism, three futuristic dogmas, were clearly expressed here and culminate in the vertical cylindrical node called the Tower of Light, the visual focus of the entire system. During World War II, a bomb extensively damaged the station, and the postwar reconstruction partially betrayed the original design, which this plan proposes to restore. The configuration of the new linear building — to be placed in front of the station to complete the square — and the articulation of its individual elements are based on the perceptual relationship both toward (see model of the city district urban design, fig. 5) and deriving from the station complex, according to Mazzoni's original design (model, fig. 6). The scheme (fig. 7) geometrically expresses the perceptual relationship. At the central axis of the station atrium (point A) meet the two diagonals B-A and C-A, running from the corners of the station building. The alignment of the pedestrian walkway, the bridge embankment, and the south block are on the diagonal converging in the station atrium at point D. The W-Y axis, centered on the open portico, connects the new bus station, the railroad tracks, and the underground garage, leading into the linear building atrium and continuing via the mechanized link up to the old town. The D-F diagonal axis of the walkway — sloping down from the park, passing under the old bridge, and terminating at the south corner of the linear building — converges on the axis of the station atrium. This system of alignments structures the space-time relationships between the station and the linear building and the park above, giving shape to the voids carved into the landscaped roof. These voids have a dimensional progression from outside to inside, converging on the linear volume in the form of a narrow street running between the multistory atrium of the south side and the open court of the north side. The vertical connections (elevators and stairs) and the volumetric articulation of the street space are geometrically projected on the curvilinear glazed façade of the building.

6

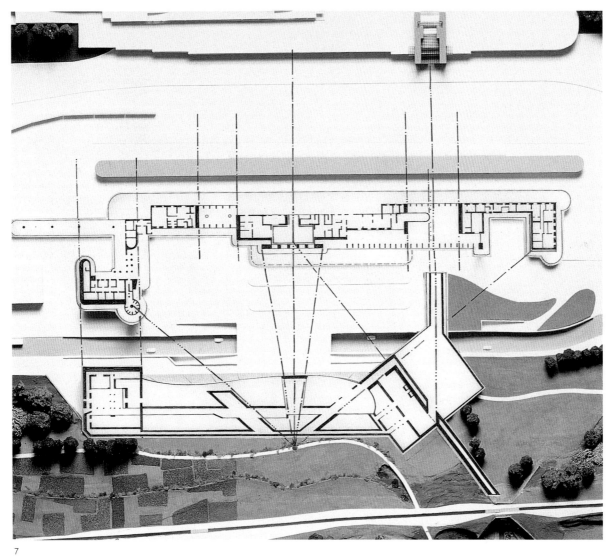

7

8. Approaching the pedestrian podium of the south block (left) with the multistory atrium connected to the curvilinear glazed façade (right).

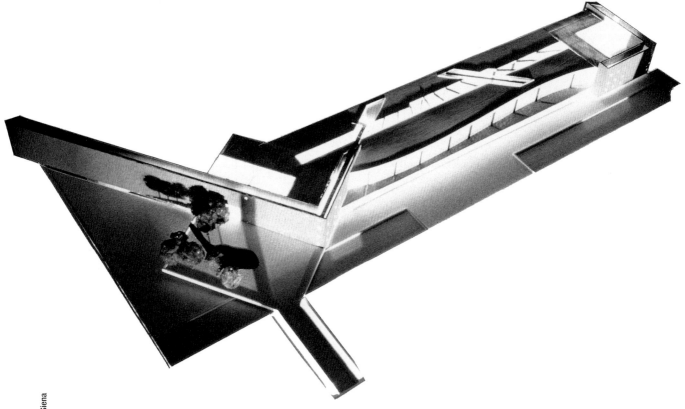

9. The voids of the linear building converge on a narrow street running between the multistory atrium (left) of the south side and the open court (right) on the north side.

10. The new configuration of the station square.

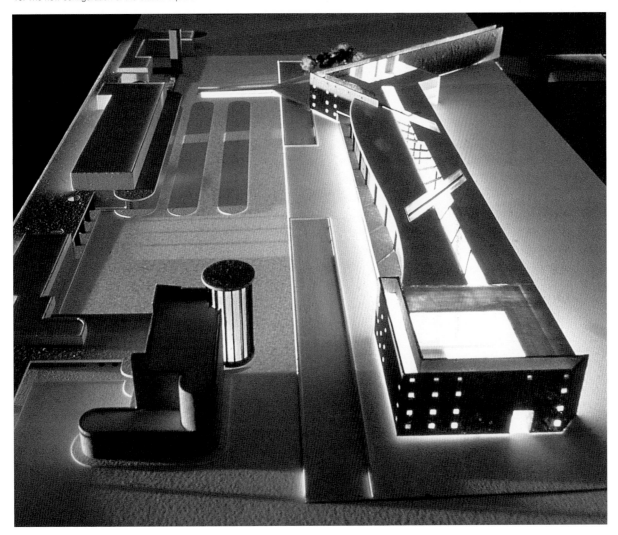

11. Life in the busy urban station node is particularly active after dark: The dynamism, transparency, and flood of light generated by the architecture of the linear building and punctuated by the restored luminosity and transparency of the station building, through which the passing trains can once more be perceived, the strips of light issuing from the underground infrastructure, and the Tower of Light itself all contribute to its powerful sense of unity.

Theater on the Bay

Opera House, Cardiff, Wales

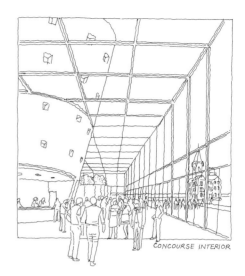

CONCOURSE INTERIOR

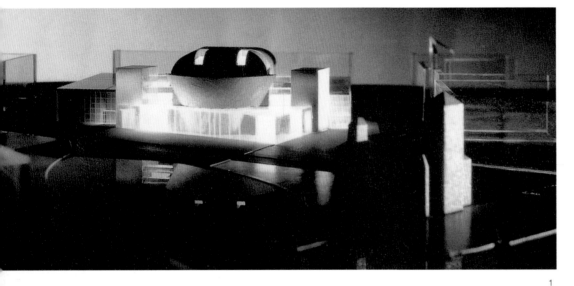

1

RICHARD REID
Building Magazine
1994

The architectural design proposed here — done in collaboration with scenographer Luciano Damiani — was conditioned by three principal concerns: the need to address the urban issues, to devise a planning strategy that allows more flexible and democratic kinds of theatrical adventures to be accommodated, to create a vivid architectural vocabulary that celebrates the post-industrial world.

The urban issues were seen as creating a vivid architectural presence in the new landscape that was an appropriate termination for the new Bute Avenue, a civic form defining the landscape space surrounding the existing historic buildings, as well as a symbolic landmark along the edge of the bay as seen across the water from Penarth and surrounding districts of the city. The sculptural forms of the curving auditorium, contrasted with the transparent angled planes of the main concourse and the expressed flanking vertical circulation, were seen as the principal urban gestures designed to create a more accessible, legible, and approachable place.

The principal theater-planning concept was the conception of a theater that replaces the traditional scheme of stage and auditorium with a more flexible and democratic kind of space unified to create greater audience participation. To achieve this, the architects have developed a theater plan functioning on three quite different kinds of levels by varying the relative positions of the stage and audience. In the first, it approximates the traditional stage; in the second, it is a kind of thrust or apron stage; in the third, it is possible for the stage to be entirely surrounded by spectators.

1. Model of new Opera House in Cardiff, Wales, with sketch of concourse.

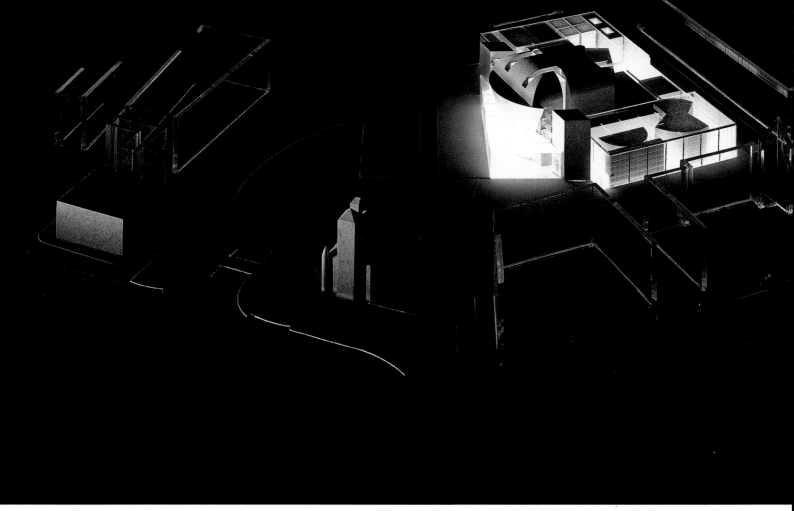

2. In town-planning terms, the scheme defines an appropriate termination for the new Bute Avenue. It accommodates the theater community in a glass-framed village environment, an urban fabric that completes the city block and responds to the different scale in density and height of the planned surrounding development.

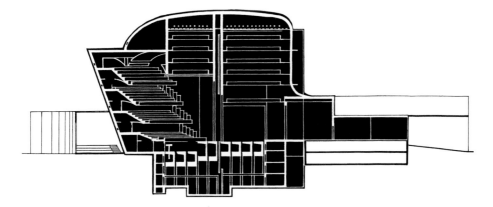

3. The stage, shown above in a cross-section of the Opera House, is located on a series of stepped platforms activated hydraulically to contoured levels as required. Two fly towers are proposed, one over the traditional stage and the other over the extended stage. The proscenium is able to accommodate opera, drama, ballet, dance, and musicals. Four tiers of seating above the stalls encircle the projecting stage, bringing the seats closer to the performers.

THE ENTRANCE CONCOURSE

This is achieved by a modular area of stage, located in the once traditional pit, on a series of stepped platforms activated hydraulically to contoured levels as required. To facilitate this greater flexibility, two fly towers are proposed, one over the traditional stage and a second, higher one over the extended stage. The proscenium is also adjustable to accommodate the activities of opera, drama, ballet, dance, and musicals that want to exploit the flexibility of the extendible stage.

The seating above the stalls is arranged in four semicircular tiers of seating climbing in a steep inclined wall encircling the projecting stage. The emphasis is on the comfort and convenience of the audience as well as bringing each and every seat closer to the performers. All this is accommodated in the tight, bell-shaped plan of the galleried seating, which combines a horseshoe-shaped central section with flanking concave wings.

Architecturally, the various parts of the theater complex are made quite distinct — the high, curving auditorium and fly towers raised above the volume of the foyer, axially designed with the principal public space enclosing the historic Head Building. This principal solid volume is flanked by vertical circulation towers with linking bridges and connecting escalators.

The entrance concourse is a wedge-shaped, transparent volume, angled to align with the main avenue and glazed to be more convivial and accessible. Behind this entrance concourse, the accommodation for the working community is located in a series of partitions and spaces of varied size creating the sense of a village framed in a glazed envelope, the building envelope here completing the city block that the theater complex occupies.

The architectural effect overall is to create an attractively light and human environment, accessible, legible, and communicable both for the public and the performers as well as the community working within the building.

Opera House, Cardiff

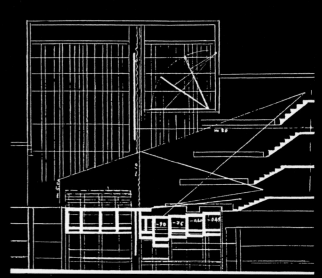

Section of traditional scheme of seating layout with raised stage, moveable transparent ceiling, and 11-by-14-meter proscenium.

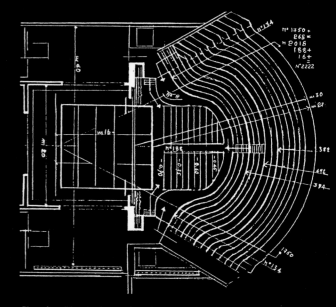

Plan of traditional scheme of seating layout with raised stage, 10-by-11-meter proscenium; including the stall area, it seats 2,038.

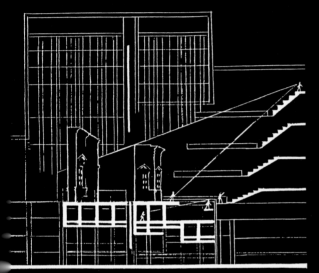

Section showing the adjustable stage for epic musicals, with a small orchestra pit, large overhead, and encircling performer's path.

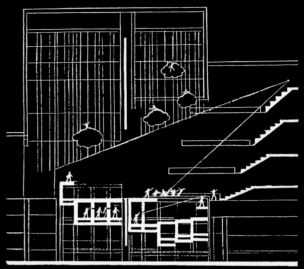

Section for Wagnerian-type orchestra. with the chorus in the stall area and an encircling performer's path.

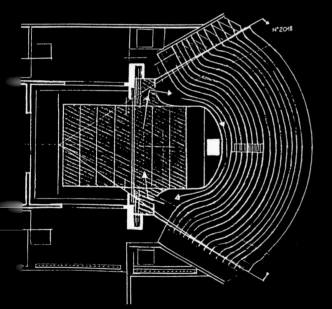

Seating 2,018, it has a small orchestra pit for Brechtian drama and a 10-by-10-meter proscenium.

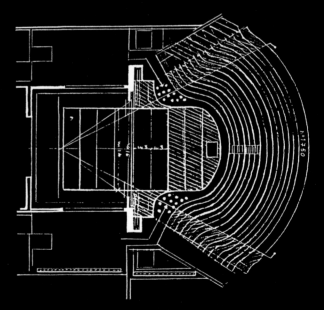

Plan showing extended overhead, which enlarges the stage area into the auditorium. With space for a Wagnerian orchestra and a 10-by-11-meter proscenium, it seats 1,750.

4. To obtain greater audience participation, it is possible to vary the relationship between stage and audience in three different ways. The diagrams illustrate the traditional stage, the thrust or apron stage, and the stage entirely surrounded by spectators.

The New Frontiers of Discovery

Italian Pavilion at Expo '92, Seville, Spain

1

ANDREA LUMINARI
Euros
March 1992

Anyone entering the Italian Pavilion cannot help being impressed: The entrance is located in the heart of the central gallery where there is an enormous globe in perfect suspension, representing the Earth as it was known before Columbus' departure. The effect is like being projected into outer space, where you can tangibly experience the Earth's rotation.

The itinerary starts from the central globe, in which the movement of the Earth's surface is represented according to Martin Behaim's world map of 1491. It continues with the geographical discoveries shown in Michelangelo Antonioni's film on the theme of the four elements of the universe, projected with modern laser techniques onto the vault of the 100-seat auditorium installed inside the globe.

While this represents the past, the theme in the gallery continues with the present and future: Suspended near the earth is Leonardo's large flying machine as testimony to the conquest of flight and to the possibility of levitation beyond gravity — man's first great conquest after his journey inside the planet. And where is this flight directed? Toward the moon — a second suspended sphere with a satellite in its vicinity. The moon looks very much like a luminous TV station regaling its audience with images of its hidden face, the proof of what new technology is able to do: show us what we cannot see from Earth.

In the part of the gallery concerned with the future, with what we have not done but will soon be able to do, we have the red planet Mars and a model of the Vela Italica. This is a new kind of satellite that absorbs energy from the sun's rays to propel it like a sailboat through space without the need for any energy for thrust. This satellite is not theoretical and has been adopted by the European Union as the basis for a project that is undergoing further studies in the European space-research centers.

Another integral part of this scenario is a catenary cable that runs diagonally across the gallery; attached to the cable is a special mobile gold-plated object. Simulating the space-time sequence of the sun's movement, it starts out very small and high up, gradually picking up speed and expanding to maximum size as it reaches the lowest point. When it is struck by the laser beams, it lights up and its shape clearly recalls Giacomo Balla's futurist drawing "Mercury Facing the Sun." This moving object has a dual function: first, as an integral part of the general solar-system theme and then as an exhibition device whose pendular movement draws the visitors' eyes across the whole gallery space, as they search for the full meaning of the *mise en scène*. Despite the effective solution of the catenary cable and the magical aura of the exhibition design, it still remains rather complex and is not always easy to follow.

Sartogo, a past master in World Expo designs, replies: "Communicating science is a difficult task, as science itself is a complex and often cryptic subject, so it is only natural that an exhibition of this kind should reflect this. What is important to me is that the exhibit offers diversified levels of interaction. On entering, the visitor is attracted by what catches the eye. Then if he wants to know more, he can analyze the data displayed and interact with them. For a more thorough understanding, he can study the catalog."

1. Rotating globe suspended over the heads of visitors to the Seville Expo '92.
2. In the middle of the gallery, the Earth is seen as it was represented before Columbus' departure. Inside the globe a film directed by Michelangelo Antonioni on the theme of the four elements of the universe, a sophisticated interplay of sound and light, is projected onto the vault. On the lower left stands a Renaissance statue of Atlas from the Farnese Collection.

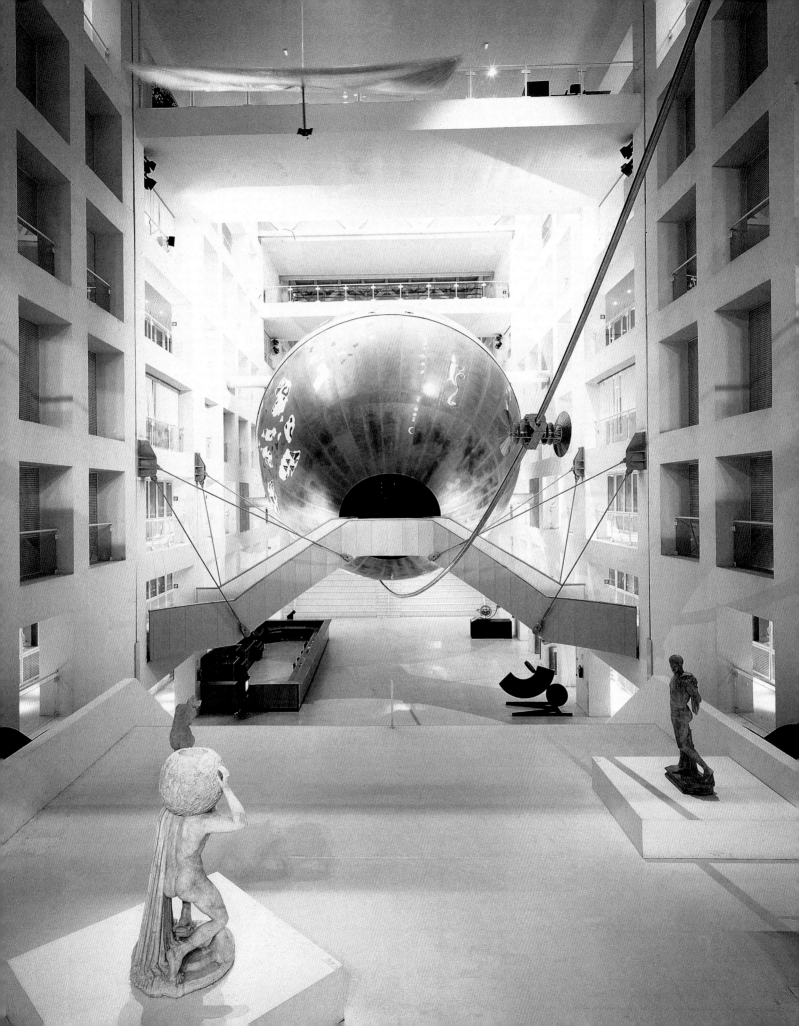

3. Model view of the grand reconstruction of the solar system with the hidden face of the moon as revealed by today's space exploration (right) and the new frontier of Mars (left).

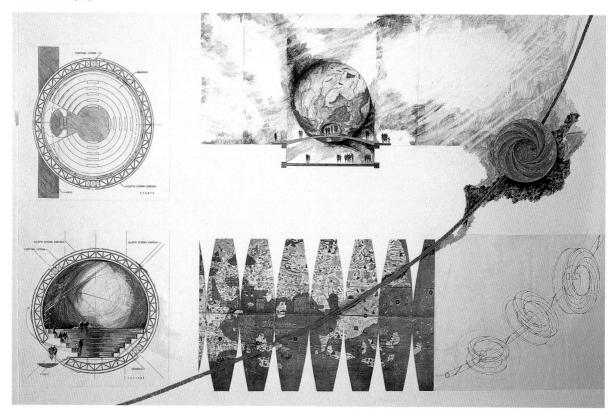

4. The surface of the Earth, as represented on Martin Behaim's map of 1491 (lower center), the 100-seat auditorium inside the sphere of the planet Earth (upper and lower left), and the pendular catenary cable simulating the space-time sequence of the sun's movement (right).

5

GIAN PIERO IACOBELLI
L'Arca
October 1992

When Ulysses passed over the Pillars of Hercules, the great divide between past and future was established, perhaps for the first time in the cultural awareness of the West. How long after the meeting of Columbus' followers with the American Indians did speculation about their biblical origin (regarding the nature of the indigenous population and how they had come to this far-off land) continue, while the natives themselves, strangely, interpreted the arrival of the European conquerors as the prophesied return of their cultural hero, Quetzalcoatl, the feathered serpent? And for how long did Galileo's telescope constitute the umbilical cord between Earth and sky or, better still, between a firmament that still circumscribed the Earth and an Earth that had finally embarked on its celestial orbit?

It was no accident that the exhibit's large central gallery became our "looking glass": the solar system that has always been the affliction and delight of wingless humankind, which searches the horizon in the hope of finding itself. By showing an Earth prior to Columbus, a moon in the wake of space missions that have revealed its hidden face, a Mars red with the fire of desire, the architects of the gallery have represented the dramatic and solicitous conflict between aspiration and power, between the real and the imaginary.

5. A bridge leads to the auditorium of the Italian Pavilion.

Car Display Device for Nissan

Nissan Auditorium, Conference, and Exhibition Center, Rome

1

RICHARD REID
L'Arca
April 1993

A compositional plan is based on the plurality of surfaces, on the parallelism of the arrangement of component parts and the volumetric articulations that define space.

This conception is deeply rooted in Japanese building culture and tradition; it is a constant that highlights spatial continuity by establishing very precise sequences of perception. In general terms, each space opens onto an adjacent one and vice versa, penetrating illusory diaphragms, which constitute backdrops to suspended elements that float in the space itself. We could refer to numerous examples: from the more complex Katsura Palace in Kyoto to the minimalist garden of Ryomi, where the modest surrounding wall functions as a backdrop to a carpet of pink sand upon which float islands of black rocks. This microcosm, due to the graded sequence from small to large (seated observer, sand and rocks, wall backdrop, trees outside the wall-sky), becomes the cosmological synthesis from an infinite universe.

Through the absolute essentiality of symbols, their juxtaposition in a hierarchical order, their dislocation according to parallel progressions, an illusory dilation of perception is obtained from the spatial cavity of interior spaces looking onto the exterior. In this kind of building context, much importance is given to moving screens that separate one space from another: their aperture and/or closure generates hyperbolic sequences of perception according to the variety of methods being used.

Generally speaking, these were the project references for the Nissan Auditorium in an industrial plant just outside Rome.

1. Elliptical skylight over the entry to the Nissan Auditorium on the outskirts of Rome.
2. The entrance opens like a proscenium toward the outside.

3. The circular revolving stage generates the geometry of the stepped ceiling and the seating.

4. Micra car model on the revolving stage.

5. A curvilinear wall marks the transition between auditorium and foyer.

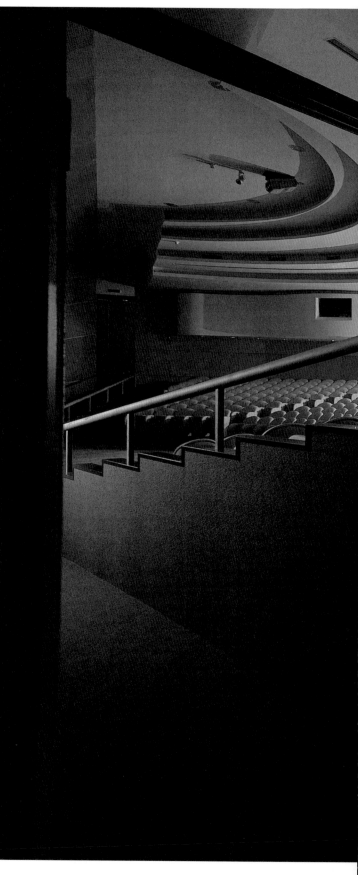

6. The foyer on two levels. On the lower left is the glazed elliptical shape of the entry. On the upper right is the curved open-close sliding wall of the auditorium.

7. Continuity between auditorium and reception-showroom is achieved by opening the back stage.

8. Sliding panels close the backstage forming a rotating circular platform for car display. The stage structure, laid out between the auditorium and the official reception-showroom, can be made to assume many configurations by combining several of its elements: a revolving circular stage; a large and/or diaphanous screen that is lowered from the proscenium lintel; slide-away wings in the wall enclosing the forestage; sliding two-paneled wall that closes off the semicylindrical backstage, which, when open, affords a continuous view of the auditorium and showroom.

730 Fifth Avenue

Bulgari Store, New York

1

PAUL GOLDBERGER
L'Arca
April 1990

This design indulges in no simple tricks like crude details at one end and refined ones at the other. Instead every point shows us how hard and tough natural materials make a kind of poetry. We see vast chunks of marble set as freestanding walls, so high they proclaim their strength, yet carved with a grace that makes them as delicate and sensual as a flower.

The store stands at the corner of Fifth Avenue and 57th Street, as critical a retailing intersection as there is anywhere in the world. It occupies the major portion of the ground floor and first level of the Crown Building, a 1924 skyscraper designed by Warren & Wetmore that is among New York's most warmly liked, if not profoundly admired, eclectic towers. The sumptuous classical palazzo of Tiffany & Co. is directly across Fifth Avenue, while the gentler chateau of Bergdorf Goodman is across 57th Street: All told, Piero Sartogo and Nathalie Grenon were faced with a formidable architectural context.

To make architecture in any street-level shop is not easy, let alone in one as laden with high expectations as this one. Not only is it urgent that the design of any retail space not overpower the objects on display, there is also the assumption that it will relate in some way to the larger building of which it is part, and make some gesture to enrich the street as well. The simplest way to satisfy all of these needs is usually to give up any pretense of strong architectural identity, and retreat into neutrality: discretion as the greater part of architectural valor.

This shop by Piero Sartogo and Nathalie Grenon stands as a reminder that it is possible to create a strong architectural presence that, instead of conflicting with the conventional demands of a retail establishment, actually supports those demands, and even enhances the experience of shopping. The Bulgari shop enters the small category of serious attempts to bring architecture to the realm of store design, taking its place alongside Hans Hollein's Schulling shop in Vienna of 1974, George Ranalli's First of August store in New York of 1976, or the long series of efforts around the United States by SITE for Best Products.

1. A monumental mass of stone forms a segmented pediment.

2. The front entrance to Bulgari, conceived as a monumental composition of superimposed layers of glass and stone.

3. View of the façade on 57th Street, where the marble portal stands as the cornerstone of the solid elements. These elements gradually withdraw to leave space for the voids as the building retreats from Fifth Avenue, revealing the interior gallery projection onto the street.

Bulgari, New York

5

4–6. The vaulted arcade has all the aura of a galleried hall (fig. 6) flanked by *botteghe* (fig. 5). The articulation of the vaulted surface marks the transition between the gallery and the adjacent spaces (fig. 4).

GLASS LAMP

An elliptical silk shade intersected by a plane of glass with beveled edges. When lit, the edges form a square of light.

TIFFANY & CO. TABLEWARE

Piero Sartogo and Nathalie Grenon combine in their designs a strong intellectual orientation with a unique sense of scale and visual perception. Their stylish approach has yielded a highly original, yet practical tableware collection. The objects are manufactured by the Austrian crystal company Riedel.

The crystal bowls comprise half-spheres and cones that rest on separate cylindrical bases of compatible proportion. Each style is available in three sizes, 9.5", 12", and 16". According to John Loring, Tiffany design director, the Sartogo/Grenon collection represents "a highly original, structural approach to crystal design. The strong visual presence of these pieces results from calculated tensions in the architect's interplay of solid and not-so-solid geometry." Transparence and reflection play their traditional roles in Sartogo/Grenon crystal with expected brilliance, while the at once simple and audacious structural balance of each piece affirms that there are still new territories that can be legitimately explored in the ancient field of glassmaking.

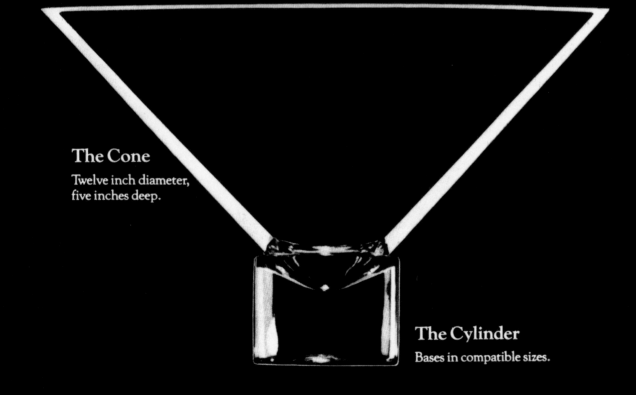

AUDI CHAIR

Like an elastic band, the back of this chair accommodates
the movements of the body and bends with it. Metal-spring
structure, fabric cover, laminated birch wood.

DIAMOND CHAIR

The front legs, which go on to form the arms, and the back legs are made of either natural or ebonized walnut. The one-piece molded steel body of the seat and back is padded with polyurethane foam and covered in leather. The suspension is achieved with steel springs.

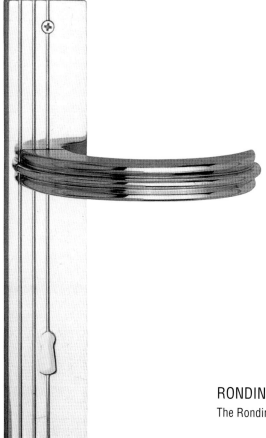

RONDINE HANDLE

The Rondine handle is shown with some of its variants for doors, windows, etc.

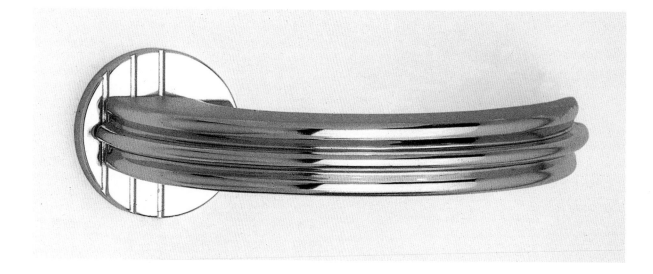

ALA CHAIR

A raised, straight-backed armchair for reading and writing. Ala is a system with standard arms and variable settees, seating one to four people. Upholstered fabric, cherry wood.

Kekkai

Bulgari Showroom and Office at Zenitaka Building, Tokyo

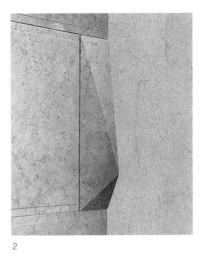

2

Until about 120 years ago, when Tokyo was still known as Edo, the Akasaka and Kioi-cho areas were surrounded by the outer moat of Rdo Castle. The stately homes of the Kishu and Owari districts and other territories belonging to the ruling Daimyo family were situated in these areas. Each spacious plot embraced a mansion with an elaborate garden. The surrounding walls and beautiful grounds, landscaped by artisans with engineering expertise, displayed those styles appropriate to the culture of that era. Some of them still grace the Tokyo area today, focal points in a greatly changed environment.

The Bulgari store in Tokyo, designed by architects Piero Sartogo and Nathalie Grenon, has recently opened in this historic and artistic center. By shaping stone with their dynamic techniques, the architects have created a space that is characteristic of their very personal style and resembles their much-admired stores in Rome and New York. The dramatic exterior is reminiscent of stone sculptures, and the spatial design seems to extend from the interior to the very outside of the building. The rhythmic play of light and shade created by the bold cut of the marble makes for an ever-changing façade as it reflects the varying

TOSHYUKI KITA
"Kekkai," Arca Edizioni
1991

1–2. The huge portal of the entrance to the Bulgari store in Tokyo cuts the corner diagonally and projects onto the lateral façade (fig. 1). Converging on the edge of the corner are the "perspective" planes of the two fronts, indicating the rotational movement of the view. The jutting blocks of the stone face vary in size and projection, according to the intervals of the perspective (detail in fig. 2).

intensity of the sunlight. The asymmetrical entrance, which defies the prevailing preference for parallel lines, represents the world of sculpture. A spatial design devoid of parallel lines; a combination of different materials; a powerful mass of marble.

The Bulgari shop in Tokyo, whose interior consists of finely worked cherry wood and pure white walls, is an elegant combination of variegated spaces and materials. The spectacular extent of the store is the expressive key to a dynamism that has never been seen here before.

And as such, this seems to be in keeping with the city, since Tokyo, too, boasts a multitude of faces. It changes, showing adversity of shapes with a medley of irregular angles and viewpoints. Furthermore, a subtle difference in coloring of the same natural wood separates the shop's interior from its exterior.

The combination of powerful vertical and horizontal lines, devoid of parallel directrixes, produces a vibrant yet peaceful atmosphere. Sartogo creates space by expertly cutting boundaries out of stone. By combining and designing volume and space, Bulgari of Tokyo expresses images that differ widely from the ones Sartogo has used before: wood and stone, Italian and Japanese traditions, the impression that things are smaller when viewed from a distance, as inspired by the stone gardens of the Ryoanji Temple in Kyoto — this is a similar method in that it expresses natural creations while guaranteeing both extension and depth to space. When Sartogo designed this store, he must have been inspired by the work of those artisan-craftsmen who built the ancient walls of Kioi-cho in Tokyo and the architecture of Rome.

There is a method called "Kekkai," which is a means of separating space in a spiritual way, without using boundaries. Sartogo and Grenon have skillfully adopted this traditional awareness of space: — harmony of East and West, the incorporation of two spaces, a combination of wood and stone, high technology used in areas such as lighting and mechanization — even though this is not shown on the surface of the natural materials employed. In conclusion, we have before us the combined wisdom of both ancient and modern people.

4

3–4. The gallery is in perspective. With their incremental intervals and dimensions, the tracings in wood on the floor indicate the fields with a meticulously burgeoning design demarcated by the articulation of the massive walling (fig. 4). The sloping ceiling with its embedded recesses accentuates the perspective, creating a composite passageway of rooms on the perimeter. The grid network, marked on the floors, walls, and ceilings by tracings in sycamore wood, by contrast measures the fitting in of perspective (fig. 3).

Bulgari, Tokyo

Future Takes Command at World's Fair

Italian Pavilion, Tsukuba Expo '85, Japan

BRUNO ZEVI
L'Espresso
May 19, 1985

Tsukuba Expo '85 offers visitors a panorama of technological research taking place in various countries and shifting scenes of "simulations of the future," the latter being a by no means secondary objective of this undertaking. Organized over 100 hectares of land by a group of prestigious architects, including Kisho Kurokawa, Fumihiko Maki, Kiyonori Kikutake, and Arata Isozaki, this project is a public-relations operation for Japan's first satellite town, based on the British model: a "city of science."

Just back from Tsukuba, the architects commented: "Ours was a sort of digression on measurements, from Da Vinci's machines to the cyclosynchrotron. It consists of a 'continuum' interspersed and punctuated with nine 'thematic installations,' the stages in an itinerary that, from the outer ramps, cuts diagonally across the three staggered floors of the rigid container assigned to us." From this sprang a perspective marble frame for Da Vinci's inventions; a prism in half-light with Bruno Munari's large "TV totem" for biomedical experiments on the human body; a "movement vector" for time, signaled by the beep of the atomic clock; a three-dimensional joint to demonstrate the process of constructing a Mediterranean pipeline; a glass-span project, as a proposal for the reconstruction of the Accademia Bridge in Venice; a cross-section of Brunelleschi's dome in Florence; and similar sequences with sloping parallelepipeds for interplanetary probes and Enrico Fermi's and Carlo Rubbia's discoveries in physics. The exhibition creates an internal landscape of the very highest quality through a network of visual images and sound reproductions that are emblematic of a "world of intelligence."

1. A perspective structure sets the stage for Leonardo Da Vinci's technical and scientific inventions, revisited today with the presentation of three-dimensional models derived from the Atlantic Codex.

Eureka L'Europe

Italian Pavilion at Cité de la Science et de l'Industrie at La Villette, Paris

1

PEPA SPARTA
Prometeo
September 1987

The conception and architecture of the Italian Pavilion is the work of Piero Sartogo and Nathalie Grenon. We asked the architects what problems arise in communicating science and technological innovations to the general public. It is a rather complex operation that requires the translation of data and scientific discoveries into a "meta-language" consisting of signs and images. On the basis of previous experience with the Italian Pavilion at the Tsukuba World Expo and the Scientific World View exhibition in Paris, the architects worked out a design methodology based on the principle of overlapping different levels of information/communication as well as interaction. In concise terms, this means offering the visitor multiple levels of comprehension and participation. These levels, ranging from simple to complex, are catalyzed visually through thematic installations or "symbolic" images.

This exhibition underlines the Italian contribution to Eureka, the European consortium for advanced scientific research, by describing an overview of the whole spectrum of projects, their various typologies, and the enterprises taking part. The achievements already made by advanced technology are projected into a hypothetical scenario of future trends.

What distinguishes the Italian approach is the importance it gives to the development of new technologies and their productive application within the development of a harmonious welfare-state system. For this reason, the scientific information of the business world gathered in this exhibition, both in terms of research and achievements, is distributed according to its likely impact on production capacity and social and physical environmental development.

The architects have created a spatial sequence centered on a projection room surrounded by four sectors. The films projected show the four themes of the Eureka project scenario — communication, production, new frontiers, and conservation. Coming and going from the auditorium to the thematic sectors, visitors are confronted with the explicit relationship between past achievements and future trends in advanced technology. On the ground, an apparatus of trapezoidal platforms provides visual and functional support for the displays, which are made up of multiple equipment, symbolic artifacts and images, screen monitors, and interactive systems. Outstanding among these are the Mascot robot, Plato's microregulators, Michelangelo's holography, the Delta O experimental vehicle, the remote sensing buoy for marine exploration, and the Iris propulsive space module.

1. The "conservation" sector: study model used in the restoration of the equestrian statue of Marcus Aurelius positioned by Michelangelo in the center of Piazza del Campidoglio in Rome.

Contemporary Perspectives

Italian Trade Center on Park Avenue, New York

2

The new Italian Trade Center in New York stands on four levels, dovetailed into a skyscraper on Park Avenue: The atrium is at street level, with exhibition spaces of various dimensions at basement level, while the technological areas and management offices are housed on the upper floors. The composition of the project assumes a degree of unity through the use of perspective and the choice of materials. Perspective is ever-present as one passes from the street to the vast atrium on the ground floor, then to the gallery with the exhibition halls on the floor below, as it is with the vertical connections, the operational area/reception, and the multipurpose exhibition space.

This perspective mechanism stands as a constant that lends rhythm as visitors move through the center: In fact, as in Palladio's Teatro Olympico and the gallery of Borromini's Palazzo Spada, the anthropometrical dimension is based on the increase in perspective that modifies the perception of space according to one's direction (either entering or leaving). The illusionistic effects usher in a privileged view with the intention of disturbing or confusing, or even overturning, the perception of linear perspective (anti-recessionist illusion).

MASSIMO DI FORTI
L'Arca
June 1992

1. The parapet in solid blocks of stone runs along the side of the stairs leading down to the multipurpose exhibition space.
2. The space of the Park Avenue entrance to the Italian Trade Center is marked by a perspective grid traced onto the pavement. This creates an effect of spatial dislocation in the volumetric articulation of both its extension and its height.

This view goes from Park Avenue toward the far interior, ending by focusing on "Le Muse inquietandi," a painting by Giorgio De Chirico, at the back of the gallery at basement level.

On the one hand, we have the geometric progression of architectural elements set out like a framework (coinciding with the passage from one ambience to the next), and on the other hand, we have the different volumes and the geometrical form of the individual spaces leading off from this framework.

The grid of perspective on the floor determines the positioning and the sequence of the dividing walls, the beams in the ceiling, the windows in the inner and outer walls, and the curvilinear volumes of the stairs. The tier from one level to another thus develops into a juxtaposition of the forms dovetailed into the geometrical web of perspective space.

This occurs at the entrance, where a curvilinear element of statuary marble borders the stairs, projecting itself into the ambience below, as with the curved stairs, leading from the technological center to the management offices. These architectural features appear again in the details that are created using artisan-craftsman techniques with stone materials, colored plasters (with a marble effect), inlay work, and metallic components.

The unfolding of the design and the quality of detail are mirrored both in the blending of different materials (marble, glass, wood, etc.) and in surfaces and volumes of the same materials. The intimate aim lies in relating once again physical presence to a dynamic structure, thereby creating an ambiguous and indisputable linguistic expression.

The strip that crosses one or more surfaces, the frame that focuses on an entrance, and the color that fastens to a volume tend to lead all the perceptive elements — point, line, surface, mass, and space — to a dimensionless matrix that triggers a conscious memory within illusion. This leading architecture back to perception in no way means ignoring functional and sociological suppositions, but rather guarantees it an aesthetic and creative role, beyond or by means of those presuppositions.

3. A sequence of juxtaposed curvilinear profiles in stone and wood runs from the reception hall to the stairs leading to the office floors.

4

6

4. The gallery, with its curved marble walls, displays a collection of selected Italian wines and their bottles and labels.

5. Detail of cantilevered bottle stands in polished brass.

6. The bar area off the exhibition gallery, with the wine-tasting area nearby. The flooring is in gray Bardiglio marble with areas of black Marquinia, and the bar itself in Carrara and Bardiglio marble.

7–9. Parallel to the gallery is a large reception hall, with three large wooden baffle-walls hinged on one side. When rotated, they become partition walls dividing the large hall into spaces of varying dimensions. The perspective effect of the room is reinforced by the windows in the rotating dividing walls. The photographs from top to bottom represent the flow of movement.

5

7

8

9

L'Imaginaire Scientifique

Exhibition at Cité de la Science et de l'Industrie at La Villette, Paris

2

The Cité de la Science et de l'Industrie, the complex recently inaugurated at La Villette in Paris, included a brilliant Italian contribution: "L'Imaginaire Scientifique," designed by Piero Sartogo with Nathalie Grenon. The gigantic letters of the title float in the basin on which rests a huge shining steel sphere, the Géode. The letters alter the steel sphere, as a result of the mirror reflection perspective. Together with the observation system that diagonally focuses on them from the esplanade and raised walkways, the letters determine a continuous symbiosis between exterior and interior. This sign in the water, punctuated by three-dimensional elements, leads into the vast multistory hollow cavity under the projection camera of the Géode, where the exhibition route is articulated according to "theme installations."

Sartogo explains: "We have offered the visitor different levels of participation from the spectacular of the installation to the identification of themes and problems and to their interaction with data concerning the most advanced scientific research and discoveries. It is a method that enabled us to make realities communicable that would otherwise remain invisible, because they are too small, too large, or too abstract, such as molecules, galaxies, 'fractals,' and 'strange attractors.'"

Sartogo and Grenon have confronted this very demanding project with dynamic expression, translating a dense cultural program and not easily communicable contents into an organized sequence of architecturally coordinated language. The use of the image as a fascinating instrument of information forms a "world of creative experience" in which science sheds its aura of mystery and specialization and becomes a shared, enjoyable, and spoken event.

BRUNO ZEVI
L'Espresso
September 14, 1986

1. The letters spelling out the title of the exhibition float on the water and reflect on the metal surface of the steel sphere Géode.
2. Thematic installations inside the great hollow cavity of the Géode.

2

Pavilion of Light

1987 Telecom Exhibition, Geneva

BRUNO ZEVI
L'Espresso
December 20, 1987

Frank Lloyd Wright used to say that he had been born lucky, because he had chosen his parents carefully. This can also be said of the Sartogo practice that always "selects" its projects carefully, in particular those involving exhibition designs. Tied to contemporary issues, often directly concerning communication, these designs have three distinct characteristics: a) they are based on a very clear space-time sequence, which structures the configuration of the exhibition path; b) they are modern, in the way they interpret the linguistic and metaphorical potential of the themes exhibited; c) they captivate the visitor, particularly through their expressive use of color.

Every four years in Geneva the most important international telecommunications companies confront each other with new products and the results of their latest research. In the 1987 Telecom, the fifth of its kind, the Italian contribution features a prestigious exhibition design presenting the symbolic installations of 54 public and private companies — a pavilion that has aroused great interest from an architectural point of view.

The Italian Pavilion at Telecom Geneva has a very powerful overall image and a fascinating aura. The architects have succeeded in interpreting that aura of lightning magic that characterizes the shifting development of telecommunications, marking the space with circles, grid lines, and real and virtual three-dimensional forms, the latter being an element frequently present in Sartogo's work. The void between the expression of the three-dimensional forms that allude to movement and the conceptual association of them makes its physical emptiness pulsate. The sense of apprehension normally experienced in an empty space is here dispelled by the reassuring message of the forms and colors.

The theme of telecommunications is interpreted here with the imposing structure of light that identifies the main path through the exhibition area. The concept of network and infrastructure, which alludes to optical fibers, determines the architectural composition of the pavilion, which appears as a network system of exhibition modules plugged into the huge suspended three-dimensional visual indicator.

The latter is made up of circular rings and rectilinear elements of neon light, whose spacing progressively increases in size from the bottom up. This use of perspective, which visually expands the physical dimensions of the space, creates a perceptual aerial structure on a much bigger scale. The structure is made up of volumes of light and three-dimensional cubic frames that intersect the indicator at the main entrance points. The space-time sequence of the path links up the two strategic zones for public access: via escalator to the higher level overlooking the "Halle" and from the principal distribution route leading to the main public entrance.

The cultural significance of this work is evident. The theme was interpreted without avoiding its many intricate aspects by adopting the materials and methods of a computerized "network." The challenge lay precisely in adapting to this idiom, which the architects pursued with an ability already demonstrated on previous occasions, ranging from the Japanese Tsukuba Expo to the recent project at La Villette in Paris.

The result is an aerial-perspective organism that expands the real dimensions of the pavilion and enhances its presence in the vast "Halle" of the Geneva Fair. An image of Italian quality and creative intelligence. An example that should be extended to the scale of "intelligent building" and beyond, to the city and to territorial planning.

1–2. The large suspended three-dimensional sign made up of neon rings and segments determines the spatial fabric of the design (fig 2). A continuous gallery is thus created with the light, a transparent and open "inscape" that links up the two strategic zones for public access (fig 1).

Savoring the Essence

Toscana Restaurant, New York

2

When the Bitici brothers of New York (formerly of Tuscany) planned to move their well-loved and highly rated Manhattan restaurant Toscana to a new East Side location (in the "bustle" of Johnson Burgee's "lipstick building" on Third Avenue), they looked for a designer that would give them certain special qualities. They wanted someone who could produce an environment to please the eye as their food pleases the palate. Just as the best cuisine releases and highlights the essence of its basic ingredients, the restaurant's environment, they felt, must go to the essence of design, far beyond the superficial aspects of decoration. They thought, for example, of Philip Johnson's Four Seasons restaurant in the nearby Seagram Building — elegant, mystical … and architectural.

Reviewing a number of possibilities, they chose a pair of architects whose credentials (including design collaboration on the Italian Trade Center in New York) confirmed that they could produce such an environment. The two — Piero Sartogo and Nathalie Grenon of Rome and New York — were, moreover, well capable of providing the Italian point of view.

The architects began by considering the awkward shape of the given space, generous in the rear but long and narrow in the front. Placing the bar and café section in the front and the dining area and private party room behind, they used curving walls not so much to refer to the early modernist piano shape, which is certainly evoked, but to provide an abstract connecting device. The motif created by the opposition of curves and orthogonal lines is carried as a theme throughout the restaurant, in the shape of the dropped ceiling, the inset light fixture, the wood-and-marble floor pattern, the custom-designed chairs, ashtrays, door handles, and even door section. To reflect regional architectural influences, the typical narrow windows of early Renaissance Tuscany are given a contemporary interpretation in the beveled apertures that frame the unusually deep entrance doors, the doors to the prominent wine cellar, and the trompe l'oeil window that gives a romantic (even kitschy) suggestion of the blue sky beyond.

SUSAN DOUBILET
Progressive Architecture
February 1988

1. A clash of curvilinear elements characterizes the main dining room entrance at New York's Toscana Restaurant. Pear wood sheathes the curved wall. A freestanding custom-designed lamp with Murano glass counterbalances the desk of the maitre d'.
2. Custom-designed entrance doorway combining pear wood and copper with handles reflecting the logo design.

3

But the Italian design instinct does not stop at abstract forms. Sensuality and vital materiality must be present as well. At Toscana, pear wood sheathes the curved walls and alternates with ebony to band the sinuous bar, the flitches carefully chosen on the fine points of wood grain by Sartogo. Marble, "that noble and vital Italian material," as Grenon calls it, is used for tables, on the bar counters, for the trompe-l'oeil window, and for the floor. In the floor, maple strips between the marble tiles create a linear pattern that, in the center of the dining area, is reversed to become predominantly wood, to echo the piano shape in the ceiling and to be used, when occasion demands, as a dance floor.

For walls not covered in pear wood, simple painted sheetrock did not suffice. Instead these surfaces are finished in encausto, a fresco-like technique employing egg-tempera pigment applied directly to a wet plaster base, resulting in a subtle play of color that imparts a sense of depth to the planes.

Most sensuous of all the materials is, surprisingly enough, glass — Murano glass used in various ways for light fixtures. In the piano-shaped ceiling hollow above the main dining room, glass "waves" in the typical blue Murano color are suspended beneath an illuminated ceiling that gives the suggestion of a natural skylight. For wall sconces and standing lamps, opaque and clear glass are combined to form a smoke-like pattern that is extended, with magical effects, in the reflections on the wall. To create these fixtures, the techniques for glass-blowing were extended to their limits, huge (five-foot-square) molds being needed to achieve a sufficiently thin material, each square producing two fixtures.

A satisfactory acoustical environment, muted without being dead, has been achieved — despite the many hard materials — by varied ceiling heights, judiciously placed carpeting, the curved wood wall, and a suspended acoustical-tile ceiling system that, reinforcing the linear pattern of the floor, is integrated into the overall design.

3. The linear walnut strips inserted in the marble floor of the restaurant clash with the curvilinear bar surface of pear wood. The tables and chairs were specially designed for this project.
4. The asymmetrical Tuscana Chair, specially crafted for Toscana Restaurant, was presented at the 26th annual Salone del Mobile in Milan and subsequently received the Compasso d'Oro award. It has been produced for the public since 1986.

The 26th Annual Salone del Mobile

Furniture Collection for Saporiti International, Milan

EDIE LEE COHEN
Interior Design
December 1986

Great expectations precede any trip to Milan, as we still look to Italy for ideas and direction despite the strides made by our own furnishings industry. For us, the Salone del Mobile holds the promise of the new — in products, in details, in treatments, and sometimes in technology. For us, the furniture fair holds the promise of the best that there is in design, albeit design that has grown increasingly more restrained over the past two or three years. What about this year in Milan? In a word, the fair was serious. In fact, it was the most serious — from the vantage points of both products and underlying mood — that this writer has seen in the 11 years in which she has been attending.

Most elegant of the Salone's chairs was Tuscana designed by Piero Sartogo and Nathalie Grenon for Saporiti. Small in scale with a gently curved back of burl wood and an asymmetrically angled seat, the piece brought to mind elements of the 1930s. The deco curve makes a sweeping comeback in this luxuriously crafted burled-wood chair. Pair it with a mate to create a love seat.

1. Because of their asymmetrical configuration, the curvilinear burl-wood armchairs of upholstered leather can be put together to form a love seat.
2. The bent plate of wood for the chair back is produced by sophisticated technology in order to appear handcrafted. The design combines classical materials like ebonized and burl wood with leather.

Tuscana Chair

Fashion Institute of Technology

Master Plan for Fashion Institute of Technology Campus, New York

2

Progressive Architecture 32nd Annual Awards

It was in search of a new meaning for the midtown Manhattan street that the Fashion Institute of Technology recently commissioned the Design Collaborative, a firm headed by the architects Piero Sartogo and Jon Michael Schwarting, to create a design that would radically change the block of West 27th Street between Seventh and Eighth Avenues. The purpose was not to engage in theoretical urban design; the Fashion Institute had a very specific motive. West 27th Street is lined with its buildings, and the administrators of the Fashion Institute have made it clear that they would like to transform West 27th Street from a conventional midtown street to a kind of semiprivate campus.

PAUL GOLDBERGER
The New York Times
February 13, 1983

It is a dramatic proposal, not only in its architecture — about which more in a moment — but in its implications for urban design. For this plan is not just another attempt to take automobiles off the streets and turn them into pedestrian malls; those have never gotten very far in New York, and that is just as well, for they seem to go strongly against the city's grain. Rather, the Design Collaborative scheme is an attempt to create out of an ordinary Manhattan street a kind of urban square or piazza. Its purpose is to make West 27th Street not so much a street as a unified outdoor room.

The two architects have come up with a scheme that is intriguing in its determination to use new and essentially modern elements to try to bring a sense of place to this jumble. It is much more than the so-called street furniture that is used in remodeled streets; here, real architectural elements reshape this street. The first of these, and surely the most important visually, is a series of partial gateways or squared-off arches, like upside-down Ls, running all along the north side. They are to be made up of translucent glass blocks set within frames of deep red painted metal, with lighting inside, so that each gateway glows softly at night. The whole project does have a certain pristine Italian industrial look to it, and there is reason to question how strongly it will work, in view of the confusion of the buildings behind it. At night, when the façades of the existing buildings are dark, the lighted Sartogo-Schwarting elements will dominate, and then they will surely be able to mold our sense of place. By day, however, the shrillness of the buildings behind may predominate.

What is certain is that this scheme would not work at all if the buildings on the street were better architecturally. If there were real lyricism to any of the façades, there could be no justification for covering them with this rhythm of industrial elements. But since the dreary buildings on the street are relatively industrial and hard-edged, it is the right idea to take off from there, and to try to render a street that will respond to the pretended rigor of these sloppy buildings with some real rigor.

1. When approached from Eighth Avenue, the depth of the perceptual recession will appear greatly enlarged. The project connects various elements of the FIT campus by closing off part of West 27th Street to traffic and forming a new urban center.
2. The main entrance to the FIT complex on Seventh Avenue. The desired effect is to shorten the apparent length of the block-long street.

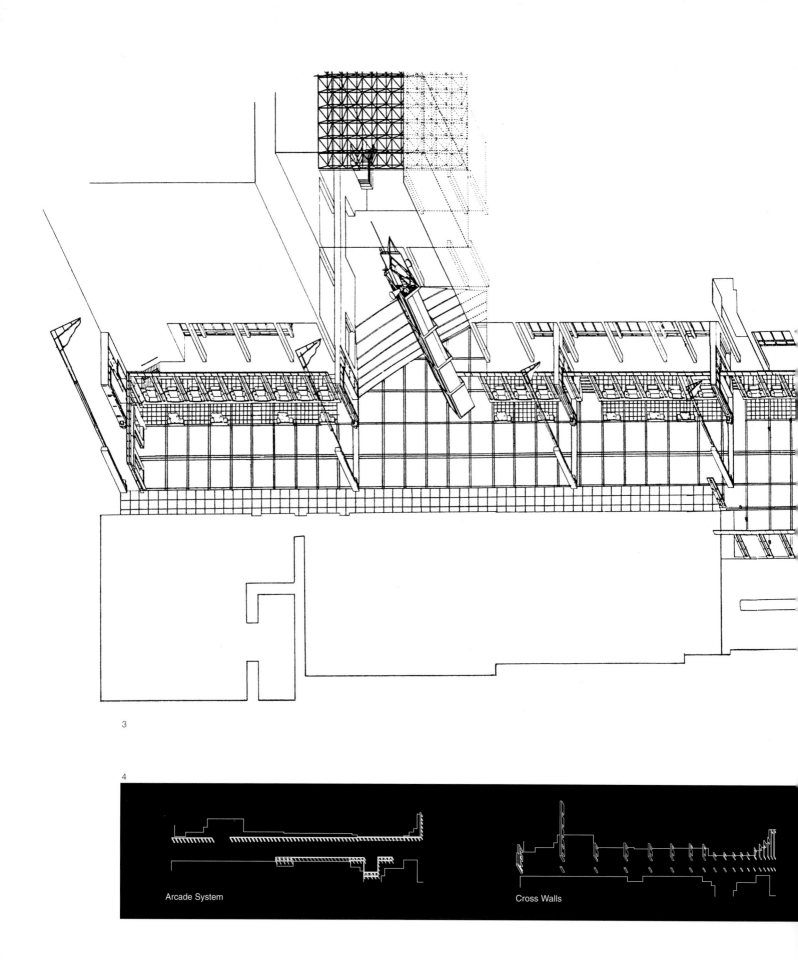

3

4

Arcade System

Cross Walls

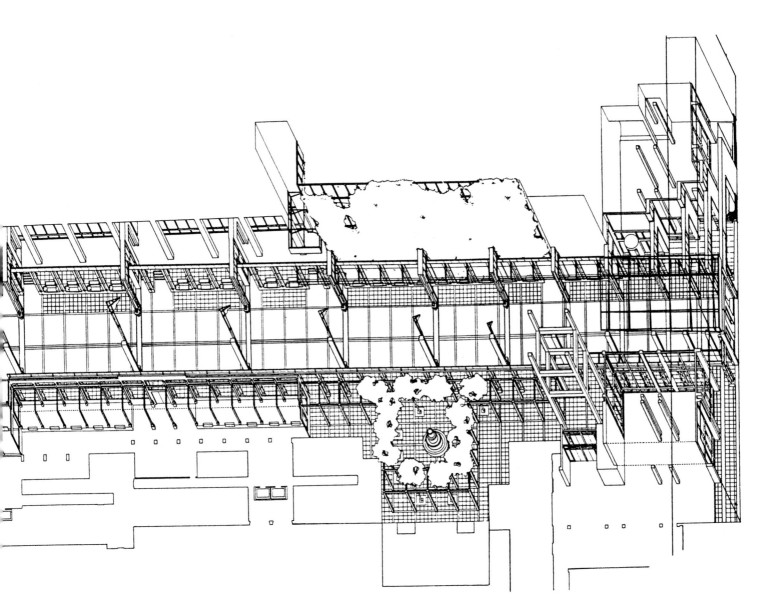

3–4. The new street space is entered through gates: Along its length are an arcade system, gates and tower, cross walls, and flag poles, all organized according to a rhythmic interval (fig. 4). This rhythm emphasizes the perceptual quality of the street. The central space is juxtaposed with more complex lateral spaces between the incidental building edges and the new configuration (fig. 3). The tower marks the entrance to the new student center and library.

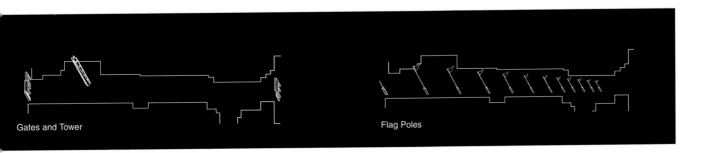

Gates and Tower

Flag Poles

Fashion Institute of Technology, New York

5

KENNETH FRAMPTON
Parametro
June 1984

It is perhaps appropriate that the rationalist order of the recent FIT complex (designed in the early 1970s by the architects de Young and Moscowitz) should be matched by an equally rational scheme developed by the Italo-American design partnership of Piero Sartogo and Jon Michael Schwarting. However, this proposed addition has been somewhat influenced by "revisionism," both the Italian, neorationalist avant-garde and the Collage City school of urban design stemming from Cornell University. While the projected scheme is a fairly convincing synthesis of these two approaches, one senses the presence of a potential split. On the one hand, there is the trabeated order (related as it always is to a sense of public order), on the other, there is the presence of a more liberal, scenographic-cum-constructivist approach toward the creation of form. This last is most apparent in the constructivist clock tower, which checks the progression through the mall and helps to turn the pedestrian toward the winter garden entry to the Alumni Plaza. Not only does this structure help to integrate the mall with the existing institute buildings, but it also alludes to the possibility for construction to be elevated to the status of tectonic form.

On the face of it, the desired effect is to shorten the apparent length of the block-long street when seen from the main entrance to the FIT complex on Seventh Avenue. The intention is to achieve this by distorting the normal perspectival perception of the receding space, since theoretically the intervals at which the places recede from the eye will be progressively countermanded by a growing increase in the intervals between the subdividing planes and by an equally compensating increase in the height of the flag standards and the size of the "frozen" flags. This is a conscious reversal of the scenographic format of Renaissance space, particularly as this reached its apotheosis in the Baroque period. The opposite effect obtains, of course, when the proposed FIT campus is entered from the other end, that is to say when it is approached from Eighth Avenue, for then the depth of the perspectival recession becomes exaggerated (à la Michelangelo's Campidoglio or Bernini's Scala Regia) and the enclosed block will appear greatly enlarged.

5. Study model indicating typical arcade section, podium, and glass cross-walls.
6. The model of the new West 27th Street as seen by night.

1. An extensive urban green area is the new environmental connecting element between the Lingotto neighborhood and the city of Turin. The architects have substituted the existing straight path of Via Nizza with a curvilinear one that echoes the course of the river bank.

Science and Technology Park

Renovation of the Fiat Lingotto Factory, Turin, Italy

2

PIERO SARTOGO
Statement
1983

The plan envisages two complementary organisms: the Technological Park — organized for development, production, and research in advanced technology — and the Forum of the 21st Century — a cultural laboratory exemplifying the indissoluble interrelations between science, technology, and industry.

Instituting productive activities of an innovative nature means setting objectives such as economic self-sufficiency, functional optimization of architectonic types, and respect for the indispensable characteristics of typological identity (as a rationally designed container of productive processes).

Instituting cultural activities of a technical-scientific nature for the general public at Lingotto means using the patrimony of an industrial civilization by projecting it into the scenario of scientific, technological, and industrial innovations.

To draw up such a plan for the reuse of Lingotto, to offer proposals regarding the expressive and functional role and image of this megastructure, means creating a strategy of development for the city and for the activities that characterize it.

2. The Lingotto factory, seen here in a 1927 photograph, took its name from a suburb southeast of Turin.

CESARE PROTETTY
Scienza Duemila
June 1984

In March 1982, after 60 years of activity, the Fiat company decided to close down its factory at Lingotto. With its machines and assembly lines dismantled, Lingotto, devoid of technological contents, remains a very significant architectonic structure, both for its grand scale and for its strategic position in the city. Fiat consulted a number of Italian and foreign architects and asked them to submit ideas and proposals regarding the future destiny of this structure.

Cesar Pelli (USA), Luigi Pellegrin (Italy), Lawrence Halprin (USA), Hermann Fehling and Daniel Gogel (Germany), Gottfried Böhm (Germany), Gae Aulenti (Italy), Renzo Piano (Italy), and Kevin Roche (USA) suggested using Lingotto as a residential development. Richard Meier (USA), Denys Lasdun (Britain), and John Johansen (USA) proposed a residential center with shops, sports, and cultural facilities, but they wanted to reserve the central volume of Lingotto for a museum dedicated to the history of automobiles and transportation sciences. Piero Sartogo (Italy) and Ettore Sottsass (Italy) proposed a science center (or "forum," as Sartogo puts it) as a point of cultural exchange, and as a research and study center. Hans Hollein (Austria) envisaged a museum of history with a gigantic hotel and three symbolic towers. Vittorio Gregotti (Italy) not only wanted to build a museum of science and industry but also to cover the whole railway area and create hills, avenues, and ponds — a sort of Torinese Champs Elysées. Roberto Gabetti and Aimaro Isola (Italy) supported the idea of a museum of advanced technology and a polytechnic, while Gaetano Pesce (Italy) preferred an institute of information technology and an ultramodern conference center. Aldo Rossi (Italy) and James Stirling (Britain) suggested a shopping center with avant-garde solutions, while Ionel Schein (France) advanced the idea of a center for industrial building for the advanced study of architecture.

Piero Sartogo and Nathalie Grenon are the authors of the project, which could become the first Italian technological park. What is a technological park? Alberto Ronchey defines it as "an area for the intensive cultivation of technical and scientific innovations," and this must have been the architects' intention for the "new" Lingotto. A rational structure that can house more than 100 production units, at a prototypical level, with 30 to 40 staff members in each one: 3,500 people in all, who can be guaranteed the maximum production, service, and advanced technological research facilities, combined with the maximum integration with the local university "brain power" and the multifunctional environment of the city. This model of technological park is entirely different from the American formula developed at Silicon Valley and along Route 128 in the Boston metropolitan area, in pleasant surroundings far from the cities with enormous distances to be covered by car: an urban model totally normal for Americans but unthinkable in Italy.

Perfectly integrated with the city and plugged into the transportation network (among other things, Sartogo and Grenon provide for an underground train station), Lingotto is a structure of one kilometer in length with two helicoidal ramps at either end linked on the top of the building by the car track used to test vehicles as they came off the assembly line. In Sartogo's plan, this mobility system would be used to move the public through the structure and transport viewers to the Forum of the 21st Century in the former press building — transformed into a kind of Epcot, a permanent exhibition, which the architects visualize as a cultural laboratory exemplifying the indivisible interrelations between science, technology, and industry.

"If the Forum of the 21st century represents an architectonic and financial venture to be carried out in phases over a reasonably long period of time," remarks Sartogo, "the technological park is by no means utopian: We can start it immediately, beginning tomorrow. The new philosophy of technological parks is substantially different today. While bearing in mind the principle of the 'agglomeration factor,' which causes a parallel and exponential growth in scientific and industrial capacity, the new trend seems to be oriented toward small- to medium-sized parks. This is the case in Minneapolis, where a technological park of relatively small dimensions acts as an 'incubator' for the emerging local high-tech industry. The integration of research and development is structurally much more important for high-tech industries than for other manufacturing industries. Since they are science-based, high-tech industries can put their innovations in scientific research on the market in the form of new products and production methods. It is not surprising that high-technology activities gravitate toward the universities. Turin already has the potential for this model of technological park."

Fiat Lingotto Factory, Turin

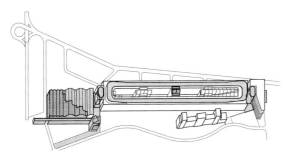

3. Forum of the 21st Century: museum circuit, records and documentation, exhibition and conference center.

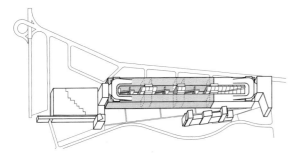

4. Technological Park: industrial production units.

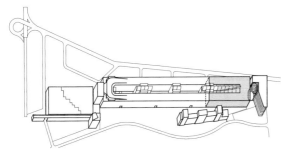

5. Technological Park: research and training facilities.

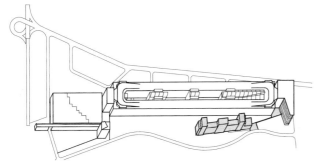

6. Technological Park: coordination and industrial promotion center.

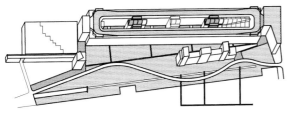

7. Urban park: sports center with jogging track, canal along former course of Via Nizza, and water basin.

3–7. Diagrams showing the allocation of functions in the reuse of the former Fiat factory.

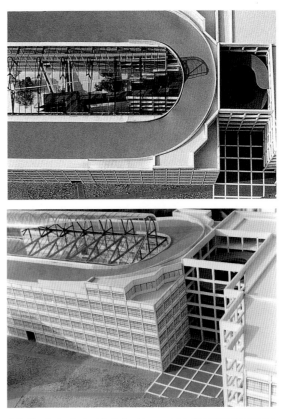

8–9. The Technological Park, the Forum of the 21st Century, and the urban park interact in the polyfunctional spatial continuum made up of the multistory atrium and adjacent gallery, the helicoidal ramp, and the mobility conduits.

10. The interior courtyards, transformed into acclimatized public spaces, are punctuated by the new mobility conduits, which multiply the functional and spatial relationships.

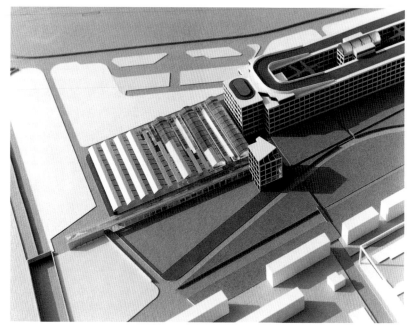

11. The water basin, canal, and the new tower form the compositional joint between natural and artificial, between the new urban park and the Forum of the 21st Century.

12. The new curvilinear path of Via Nizza, in place of the original straight one, modifies the former static frontal view of Lingotto to a dynamic polycentric one, emphasizing the spatial dynamics of the new configuration.

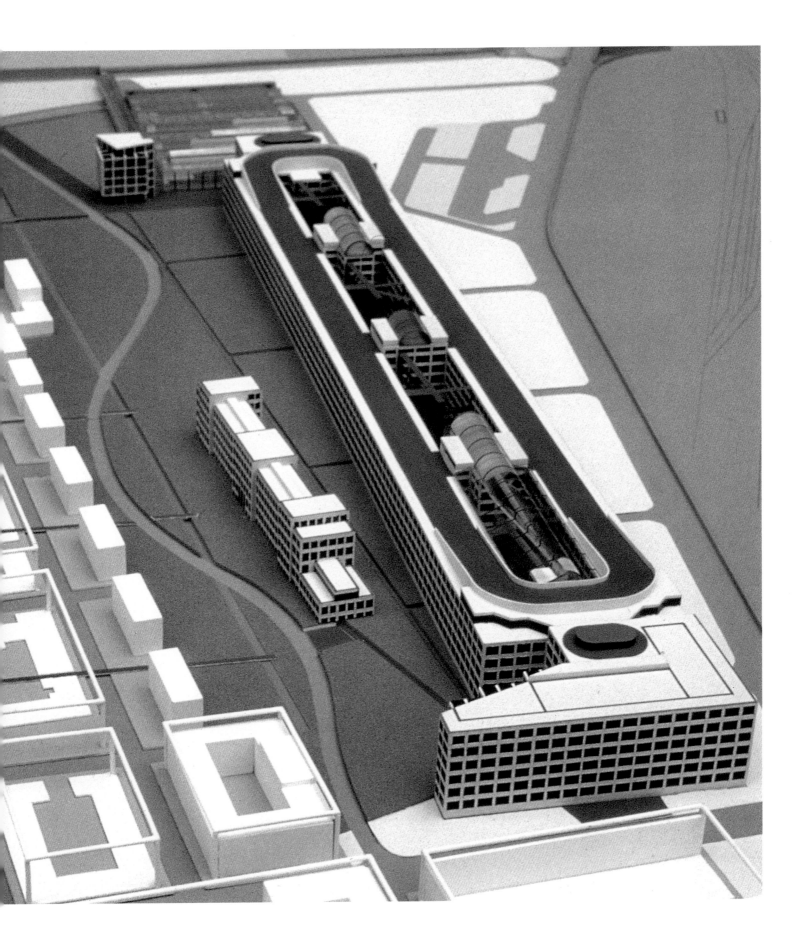

Mind Over Materials

Italian Trade Center on Park Avenue, New York

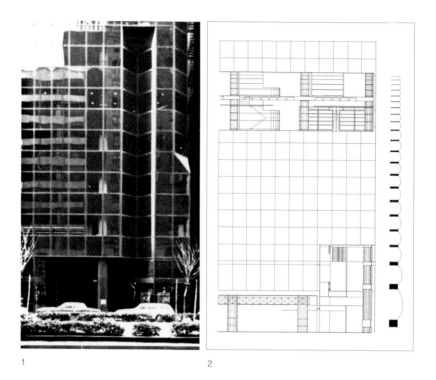

1   2

SUSAN DOUBILET
Progressive Architecture
August 1981
When a clear set of generating strategies — intellectual, verbal, diagrammatic — locks horns with the daring sensuality of materialism — the Italian passion for experimentation and juxtaposition, the American fascination with industrial products — the result is bound to be provocative. It may also be problematic, if the intellectual ideas are not consistently resolved. Hence the multifaceted nature of the Italian Trade Center designed by Piero Sartogo and Jon Michael Schwarting on four floors of a new I. M. Pei & Partners–designed office building on New York's Park Avenue.

A Tale of Two Generating Strategies

The tale, as told by the architects, is simple enough, involving two strategies. One strategy identifies each floor with respect to its vertical location in the tower, by drawing horizontal bands of varying widths across columns and other elements. On the lowest floor, the bands are wide, with wide, intensely colored spaces between them. They become narrower and lighter in tone as one ascends the building. The second strategy reinforces the diagonal implications established by the given building envelope's chamfered surfaces. This diagonal movement is expressed in various ways: by stepped walls, by straight and curved diagonal walls, by diagonally oriented ceiling and floor elements, and by a curved diagonal edge to the suspended ceiling in some areas.

1–2. The Italian Trade Center is located at 599 Park Avenue, in a building designed by I. M. Pei (fig. 1). The progression of stripes is a unifying device that establishes a continuous spatial sequence throughout the four separate floors of the center. Bands diminish in width, spacing, and color intensity as one ascends through the building, as seen in the section (fig. 2).

The Tempest of Expressions

Within this fairly simple ordering system of horizontals and diagonals simmers the infinitely complex world of expressive gestures acknowledging, through materials and forms, the activities of the Trade Center. These complex responses are inspired in part by the diverse nature of the functions and in part by the contradictions within the building, which contrasts the rough weight of a concrete structural system with the smooth black scalelessness of the glass curtain wall; but they result especially from the contrasting natures, personal associations, fascination with materials, and historical interests of two architects with enough energy and abandon to explore and experiment at every psychological and physical turn, leaving "system" far behind.

There is the cool sophistication of juxtaposed grays and Eileen Gray–ish aluminum in the emphatically narrow street-level foyer; the rough, punk, even decadently underground nature of the corrugated-aluminum-clad basement; the warm sensuousness of wood and curves in the fifth-floor wine library and bar; and the icily pristine elegance of gray-framed, magenta-accented etched glass in the administrative offices of the sixth floor. And there is more, as each of these effects is superimposed with other effects, sometimes to heighten them, and sometimes, unfortunately, to mitigate them.

Finale

In the Italian Trade Center lies proof of the obvious yet oft-forgotten lesson of architecture — that no verbal polemic, nor any seductive diagram of strategies, can succeed without consistent resolution. The Design Collaborative partners, with vision, talent, and energetic involvement, transformed many of their ideas into expressive, three-dimensional forms and spaces with architectural materials; but they left some ideas dangling ineffectually.

The horizontal band strategy does imprint itself as a continuous force throughout the four separate floors; and it works well, both as a primary physical element and as background for other elements, its scale changing appropriately with its use. Where it is applied subtly — in the etched glass of the sixth floor — or boldly — in the square outgrowths in the foyer — it is exciting. When its details are not worked out — when wood moldings end unceremoniously on the fifth floor — it is awkward and immature. The diagonal strategy is weakly realized as an intellectual organizer of "virtual" space. The diagonal drift can be sensed in the basement, but the low hugeness of the space is the dominant effect. The foyer diagonal perversely and brilliantly reinforces the deep narrow space, but it scarcely repeats the intended message, as it is nonorthogonal to the building chamfers. On the fifth floor, the diagonals of the "virtual" space are weak shadows of the idea and are rendered in inappropriate colors and materials. And while on the sixth floor the diagonal force returns, propelling one vigorously through the space,the elements are disturbingly compressed. Most important, however, the architects pushed well beyond the limits of their intellectually imposed systems. While they raised more issues than they could resolve, the very wealth of material is provocative. And at times, the effects are nothing short of sublime.

3–6. Details of the bands on the sixth-floor walls (fig. 3), on the curved fifth-floor stairway (fig. 4), on a column in the foyer (fig. 5), and on a basement column (fig. 6).

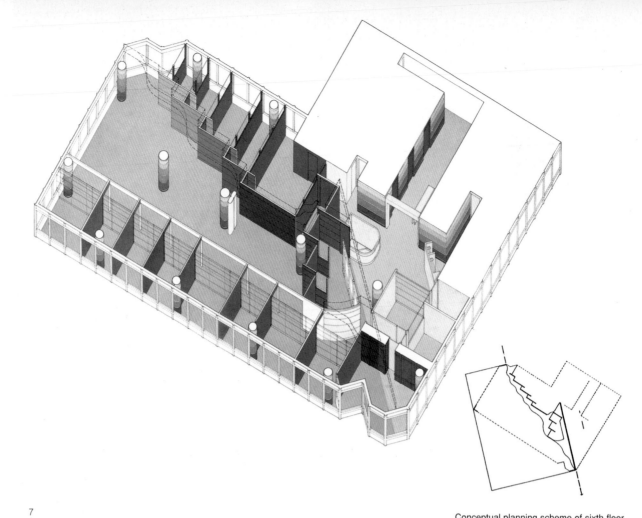

7

Conceptual planning scheme of sixth floor

8

9

7–10. Sixth-floor offices: The diagonal strategy, a response to the chamfered building envelope, is realized in diagonal walls, stepped walls (fig. 7), color and material changes (fig. 10), and curved edges of ceiling planes (fig. 9). The diagonal force is expressed in the ceiling geometry (fig. 8).

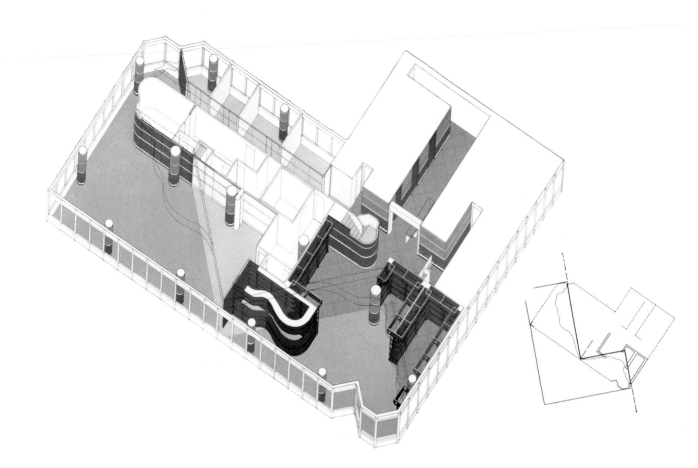

11

Conceptual planning scheme of fifth floor

12

13

11–14. Fifth-floor business and meeting center: The orthogonal layout of I. M. Pei's building is rotated diagonally (fig. 11) and manifested by "virtual" planes (fig. 12). Between these "virtual" planar surfaces and the curvilinear edge (fig. 13), the building infrastructure is revealed through "fissures" (fig. 14).

14

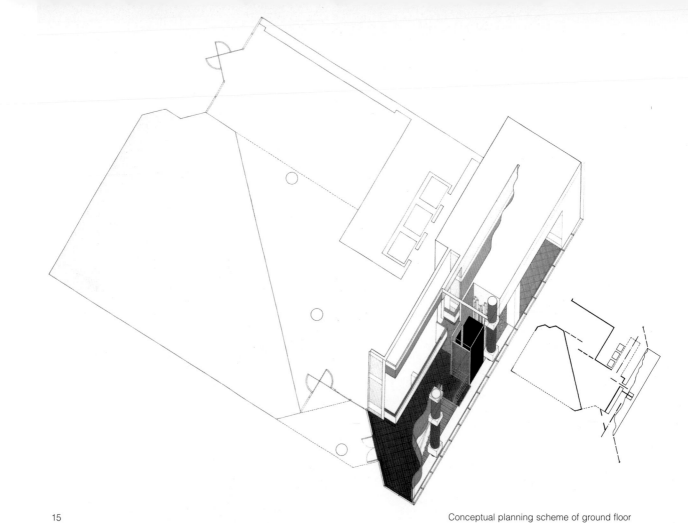

15

Conceptual planning scheme of ground floor

16

15–17. Entry level on Park Avenue (fig. 17): The vertical plane intersecting two floors is placed on the axis of the elevator, producing a visual connection between the entry floor and the lower-level exhibition gallery. Curvilinear surfaces "interpret" the diagonally opposed corners within the L-shaped block (fig. 15). A dramatic stairway and an elevator connect the lower level to the entry level (fig. 16).

Italian Trade Center, New York

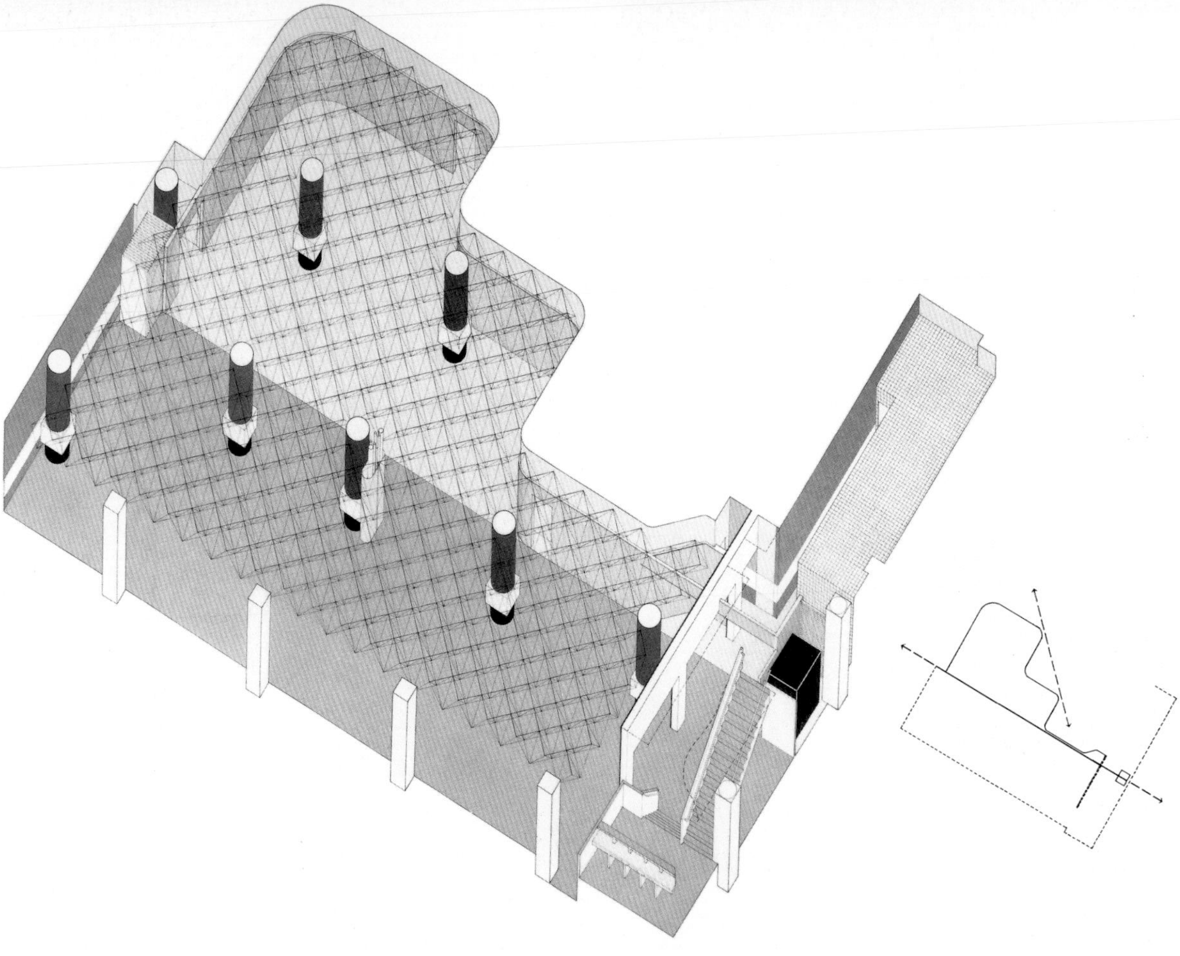

18

Conceptual planning scheme of lower leve

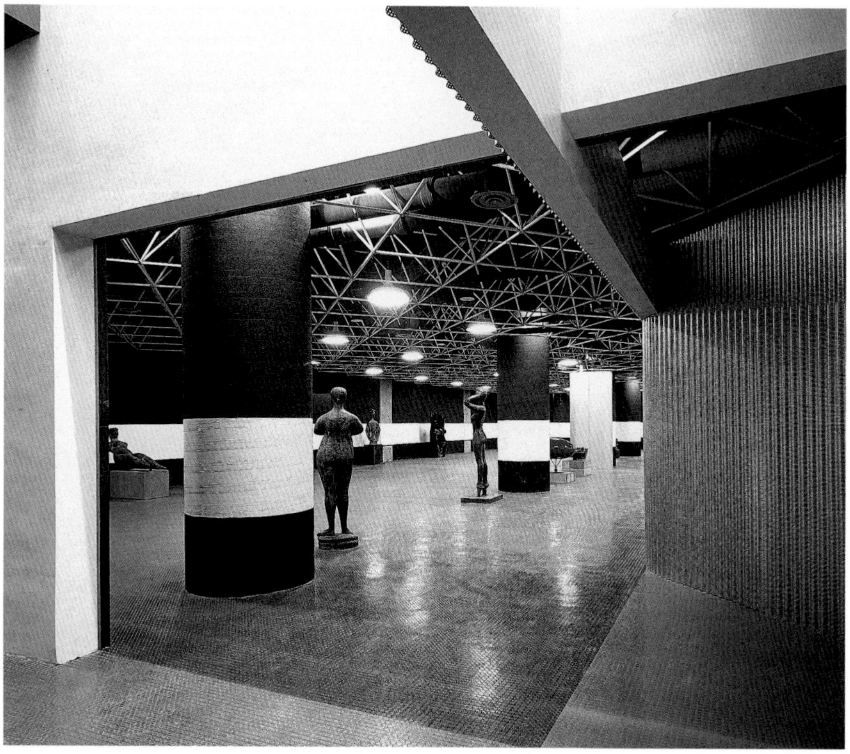

19

18. Lower-level exhibition gallery: The vertical "virtual" plane connecting the lower and entry levels is experienced through the movement of the open elevator.
19. Corrugated aluminum surfaces clash with the sleek space frame of the lower-level exhibition gallery.
20. Foyer leading to the exhibition gallery.

Italian Design on Display

Italian Re-Evolution: Design in Italian Society in the Eighties Exhibition

2

1

ALBERTO ARBASINO
La Repubblica
October 20, 1982

Italian architecture at its best made stylized and tapered armchairs, sofa beds, and standard lamps in a quest for images of modernity. It turned out numerous functional products, which, though truly admirable as showroom ornaments, make architects' abodes especially distressing (Fontana and De Pisis were less and less frequently on the walls, as with Simonetta and Valentino couture in the wardrobes). Other jokers, partly for fun and partly not to die of boredom, gathered heaps of quotations, as amusing as those pastiches (first in the manner of D'Annunzio, then of Joyce) that so delight university professors and their assistants in faculty meetings. Others produced "languages that illustrate languages" in exhibition designs. Still others, however, criticized the buildings that were built not to be utilized, but just to be eminently appraised in that architectural jargon that, in contemporary Italian style, is comparable to that of orthopedic or philatelic gazettes. A style that is restricted to commenting on the characteristic features and purpose of a "functional" or "brutalist" shop, and not the practical reasons why such a shop does not attract customers, serves no purpose, and fails.

This splendid new exhibition designed by Piero Sartogo and Nathalie Grenon and entitled "Italian Re-Evolution," or "Design in Italian Society in the Eighties," will soon be leaving La Jolla, California, for a long tour of the United States and Canada. It is sympathetic and attentive in its aim to provide a well-constructed and plausible image of original and temperamental Italian daily life.

1. Entrance wall of the exhibition at the Museum of Modern Art in La Jolla.
2. Various models of lamps appear together through their projected shades.

3

4

When excavating an ancient site, objects from the mysterious past come to light. The archaeologist tries to restore the object to its pristine state, to understand what it is. The historian finds a connection between this object and others, both before and after its discovery. The anthropologist is expected to answer the question: Who made and used this kind of object, and how did he live?

Architects Piero Sartogo and Nathalie Grenon, in collaboration with Giulio Carlo Argan, Bruno Zevi, Fabio Mauri, Umberto Eco, Gianpaolo Fabris, and Demoskopea have put the excavations of contemporary Italy on view. Opened last week at the Museum of Modern Art in La Jolla, California, their exhibition creates the strange feeling of visiting the present from a faraway observation post, as if there were, as in Borges, a kind of double reality, a time machine in which two equal ages stare at each other. In choosing between indoors and outdoors, indoors wins when we are talking about the main rite of the evening, television. And this is the moment when the Sartogo exhibit makes another brilliant qualitative leap. In it, we can see both ugly and beautiful televisions, as the Italians make them and buy them, and as architects design them (compared to American sets, those in Italy are generally more attractive, even those with far-out designs).

But then there is an ingenious turn. Televisions substitute for the heads of many mannequins and figures dressed as football players or fashion models. This is not the celebration of an Italian obsession (according to Demoskopea, a research organization, Italians on average watch television for four hours a day, two less than in the U.S.). The trick conjured up by the designers of the exhibition reveals a sort of Freudian "transference" that takes place between the Italian viewer and his TV screen. It is an ambiguous relationship that explains, at the same time, the close bond and the harsh criticism of an audience that even after 20 years has not remained passive. There are too many passions and opinions among people on this side of the set for that transference to take place automatically.

"This is not an exhibition of things," explains Sartogo, "it is the relationship between things and the people who use them every day." In the San Diego museum, the architect and sociologist put all the possible data into the hands of the exploring visitor, then they step aside and let the visitor do the work.

FURIO COLOMBO
La Stampa
September 28, 1982

3. A Ferrari, the dream car of Italians, is shown here in juxtaposition to a loveseat, symbolizing another fundamental Italian passion.
4.The Italian obsession with soccer is interpreted in the exhibition by a path framed by soccer nets, behind which are mannequins dressed in different Italian team uniforms. The mannequins have TV monitors in place of their heads, emphasizing soccer's nature as a spectator sport.

1

Who Betrayed Brunelleschi?

Brunelleschi Anticlassico Exhibition, Florence, Italy

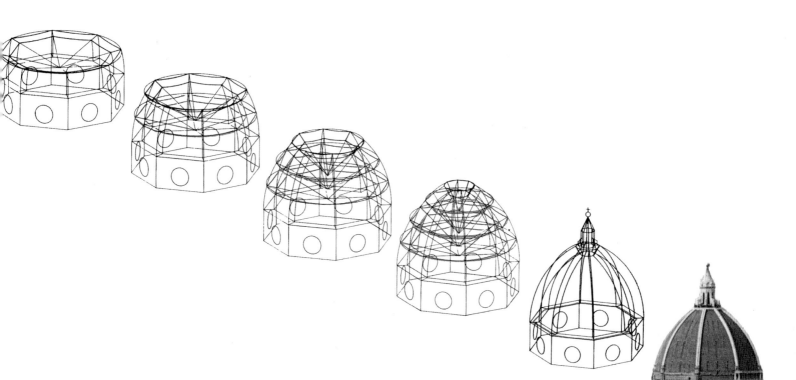

2

BRUNO ZEVI
Cronache di Architettura
1978

Florence. All over the city are bright red signs that, starting from the cloisters of Santa Maria Novella, nearby streets, squares, sidewalks, and churchyards, cluster around the cathedral and cross over the Arno, where they branch out toward the Brunelleschi monuments. Against the night sky and Florentine panorama, rays of light pinpoint the rising outlines and poles of concentration that Brunelleschi imprinted on Arnolfo's urban plan. Even the army's photoelectric apparatus is involved in the festive, exhilarating adventure of the "Brunelleschi Anticlassico" exhibition designed by Francesco Capolei and Piero Sartogo.

This undertaking is of exceptional significance in that it documents, for the first time in the six centuries since their conception, the authentic images of a genius who was absurdly "corrected," mortified, and betrayed by the mediocre and cowardly executors of his projects. This renowned master has only today recovered his identity, and his overwhelmingly anti-Renaissance message is shocking even for experts in the history of architecture.

Let us take a quick trip through the exhibition sequence. At the two entrances, next to Santa Maria Novella and the square in front of the railway station, we see the huge "indicator" of the critical thesis: A network of steel tubes simulates the actual 15-meter-high façade of Santo Spirito with its three doors. Superimposed on it is a three-dimensional metal structure painted in red, with the four semicylindrical volumes of the original design. On October 15, 1977, this sparked off a controversy unheard of since November 12, 1487, when a contemptible decision, dictated by classicist conformity, was made in fear of realizing a truly revolutionary spatial idea that aimed at banishing any kind of symmetry from the church.

1. Brunelleschi exhibit in the courtyard of Santa Maria Novella in Florence. The façade of Santo Spirito with its three doors is represented by a three-dimensional metal grid on which are superimposed the four semicylindrical volumes of the original design. Bright red signs indicate routes between the exhibition and Brunelleschi's monuments in the city: Santa Maria degli Angeli, Cappella dei Pazzi, Santo Spirito, and San Lorenzo.
2. The dome of Florence's Santa Maria del Fiore. The diagrams show Brunelleschi's rotational method of construction (see also fig. 7).

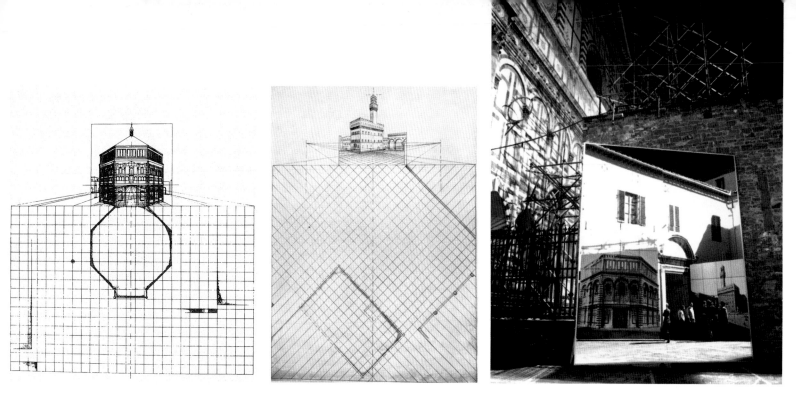

3. The genesis of perspective.

Five "stations" spell out the essential issues regarding the architectural language of Brunelleschi:

1. The genesis of perspective, symbolized by a large mirror, in which a view of the Baptistery and Palazzo Vecchio is reflected. In the Misericordia cloister, the structures of the Laurentian Sacristy and the Pazzi Chapel are interpreted in terms of their three-dimensional dynamic rotation and dissonant juxtapositions: The chapel expands visually beyond the space defined by the gray-stone framework, visible because one enters the sacristy from the corner and the center is occupied by a sarcophagus.

4. The alternative solutions.

5. The columns along the median plane.

2. The alternative solutions suggested by Brunelleschi, and the changes imposed by the clients, philologically pinpointed by Piero Sanpaolesi in 11 models, ranging from San Lorenzo to the Rotonda degli Angeli.

3. The heresies and so-called syntactical errors are presented via an explosion of colored slides viewed on diagonally positioned screens installed in the Gothic space of the refectory. In the background, there is a glowing cube cut by transparent plates that — together with the turning of the perimeter semicylindrical volumes on the façade and the columns placed along the median plane of the plan — make the gestural nodes of the Santo Spirito comprehensible.

6. Intersecting visual surfaces.

4. Intersecting visual cones, concave and convex surfaces, interiors that look like exteriors and vice versa, are part of a sequence that examines various monuments, including the buildings of the Parte Guelfa and Pitti Palace and the tribunes of the drum of Santa Maria del Fiore. On the ground, a long thick gleaming steel bar rests between the two central columns of Santo Spirito, one of them unbuilt and the other one shamefully concealed by a plain 17th-century tabernacle.

5. In the so-called Cappellone degli Spagnoli, there is a gigantic model of the cathedral dome, which demonstrates the recent discoveries of Salvatore Di Pasquale. The model, 4.5 meters wide and 3 meters high, elevated 1.2 meters above the floor, can be inspected from below. In an adjoining room, a striking three-dimensional model (scale 1:1) has been constructed of the space represented by Brunelleschi and Masaccio in the fresco of the "Trinity" and its reference to the Barbadori Chapel.

7. Model showing the centrifugal process of construction of the dome. As Salvatore Di Pasquale writes, "The dome of Santa Maria del Fiore was constructed with the method of rotational cupolas. The significance of this can be clarified in the following terms: Despite the octagonal base of the cupola, the stone and bricks that make up the wall structure appear to be laid in conformity with curved beds. This particular position can be achieved by rotating a cord around a point situated on the central axis of the cupola, a point that is moved higher and higher as the construction proceeds (see also computer elaboration, fig. 1). If the cupola had had a circular base, the intersection would have been a horizontal circle. Since instead it was octagonal, the lines have resulted in a 'catenary curve.' In reality, their geometric definition is more complex in that it results from the horizontal intersection of cones and cylinders, or as they say in mathematical terms, 'quartics.'"

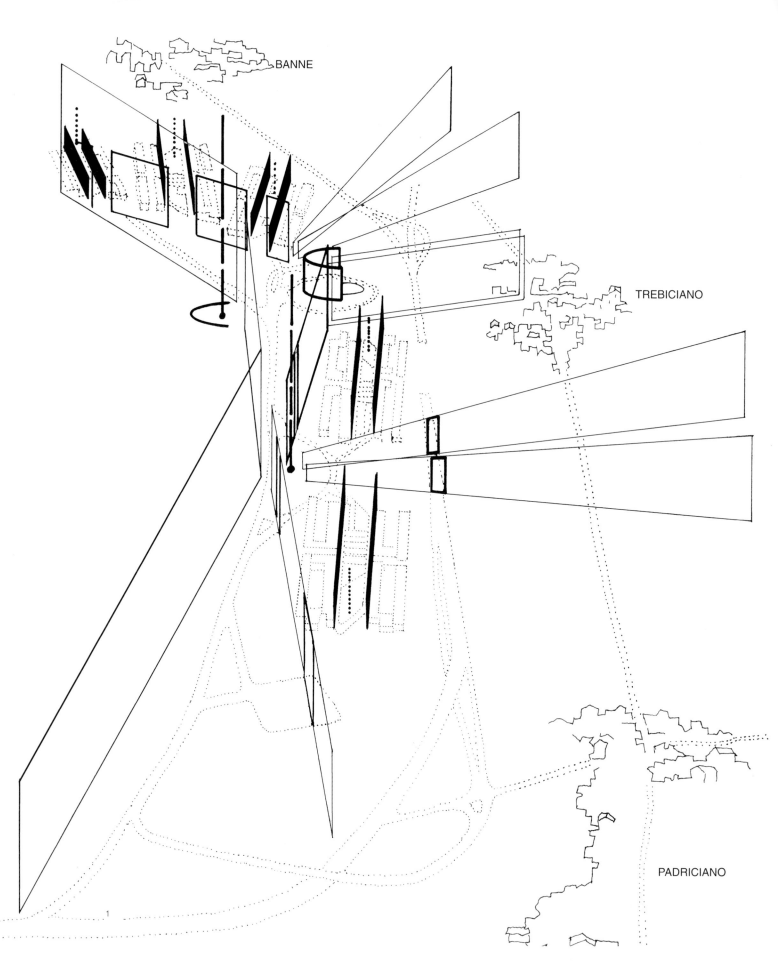

BANNE

TREBICIANO

PADRICIANO

Scientific Citadel

Master Plan for New Science and Technology Park, Trieste, Italy

2

BRUNO ZEVI
L'Espresso
May 22, 1983

Can the European Synchrotron Radiation Facility restore to Trieste its erstwhile role as the Middle European center of the cultural avant-garde and, by so doing, spark an economic recovery? This is the objective behind the formation of the "Agency for the Development of Science Park: An Area for Scientific and Technological Research," which involves not only the university but regional and state holdings as well as private enterprise.

The Banne district in the Carso hills is planned to host "the light machine": a gigantic electronic particle accelerator for the study and creation of new high-powered lasers. The 160 hectares situated between the Sistiana-Padriciano motorway and the upland park are to be used for the construction of the double-ringed structure of the "light synchrotron," research facilities, laboratories, offices for 280 personnel, residences for 140 scientists, guest rooms, restaurants, archives, libraries, convention halls, and sports fields.

A competition for a general urban plan was announced last year. Participating in it were the Milanese Jan Battistoni, Vittorio Gregotti, Roberto Morisi, and Viola e Associati; the Triestines Costantino Giorgetti, Carlo Celli and Dario Tognon, and Dino Tamburini; the Romans Sergio Lenci, Nino Milia, Maurizio Sacripanti, Maurizio Savarese, Piero and Francesca Sartogo; and also Emilio Mattioni of Udine and Aldo Padovano of Treviso. The applicants were asked to "promote the most rational and correct use of resources to create a harmonious technical-scientific community and to ensure the safeguarding of the environment and a balanced development of the local community." The results of the competition, just announced, saw Lenci and the Sartogos dividing the first prize, while Giorgetti obtained third prize.

Starting from an interpretation of their "perceptive references," the Sartogos analyzed the main roads connecting the villages, the route between Trebiciano and the "Sella Marchesetti," the topographic reliefs, and the particular vegetation of the moors in order to chart a continuum of scattered green areas; these were divided by the visual cones, hinges, and volumetric consolidation of the five "super departments" of information technology, soil chemistry, applied physics, environmental protection, and industrial experimentation. An infrastructure of vehicular access routes and supply conduits puts the complex in a close morphological relationship with the landscape, thrusting its "arteries" into the territory.

1–2. Five self-sufficient nuclei of research laboratories include environmental protection for the resource sector, information technology and telecommunications for the electronics sector, applied physics, soil chemistry, and applied industrial experimentation. The European Synchrotron Radiation Facility in Trieste is under the direction of Carlo Rubia. Shown here are its design concept (fig. 1) and the master-plan model (fig. 2).

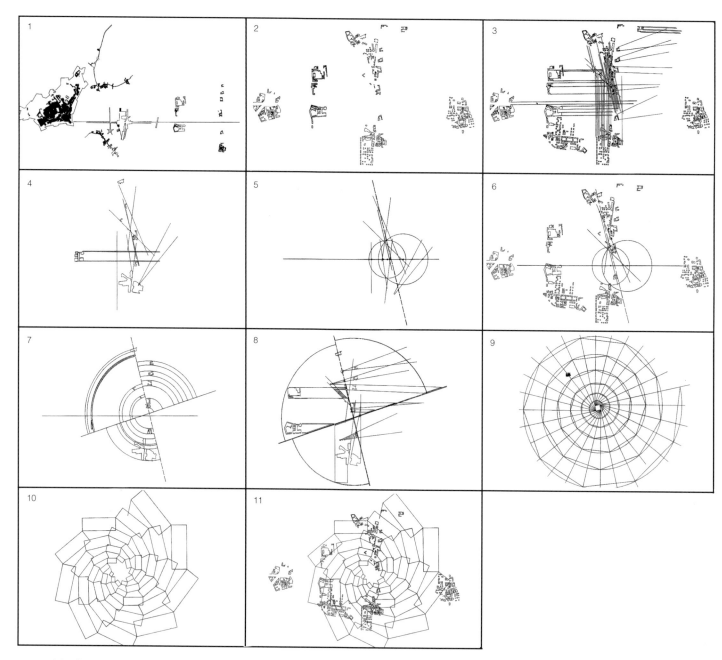

1–11. Conceptual design scheme showing the process of construction of the project-design matrix for the Bergamo district. 1. Perceptive emerging axis in the urban structure — Via Papa Giovanni XXIII connecting Bergamo Alta to the railway station of Bergamo Bassa. 2. Perceptive emerging architectonic elements in the project area — the Campagnolo-Boccaleone axis — including the old farmsteads. 3. Alignment of the urban settlements: Bergamo Alta, Bergamo Bassa, Campagnolo, Boccaleone, and Orio sul Serio. 4. Primary emerging alignments in relation to fig. 3. 5–6. Area from which there is the perception of these emerging elements. 7. Identification of specific sectors of perception of the emerging axis. 8. Areas of collision determined by the alignment of the emerging axis in reference to the sectors of perception. 9. Geometric matrix resulting from the interpolation of the areas of collision and their geometric structure. 10–11. Spatial layout of the project.

A Space of 200 Hectares

Master Plan for City District, Bergamo, Italy

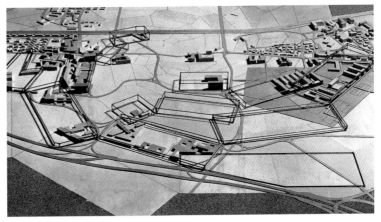

12

BRUNO ZEVI
L'Espresso
May 6, 1979

With the inauguration of this project exhibition, Bergamo opened debate on the master-plan design for a new city-district development, located between the railway station and the airport.

Piero Sartogo, who designed the master plan together with a team of 12 experts directed by Alfio Grifoni and coordinated by Luigi Bellini, remarks frankly: "It's like a room that is attached to a house when the family gets bigger. No grand gestures. On the contrary, it's done sparingly and within limits; careful not to bite off more than it can chew." One appreciates the architect's understatement, but in fact, it happens to be a particularly original and significant master plan.

The area, situated in the lower part of the city, is spread over 203.8 hectares. Wedged between the railway and the Orio Airport, it is bordered on the south by a motorway and incorporates the villages of Campagnola and Boccaleone, as well as an agricultural setting of fields and old farmsteads. The idea is to transform the area into an essential polyfunctional junction connecting the metropolitan mobility network to the city center. The most important public and private structures include a convention center, museum, and trade-fair complex, as well as offices, residences, retail outlets, and sports and recreational facilities. The organizational key to the system is the distribution of green in terms of a nursery-wood-lake sequence that is part of a large park. This park ensures a structural framework, a matrix capable of mediating between this "new countryside" and the profile of the wooded valleys to the north.

The overall image is that of a macro-organism, whose considerable physical dimensions embody the prominent outlines of Bergamo Alto and even the despicable interventions of Marcello Piacentini during the Fascist period, projecting itself over a vast panoramic radius. From the project emerge fixed values of a binding nature — "urban voids" (parks, piazzas, streets, galleries, porticoes, etc.) — and "dynamic values" — the architectonic structures where there is considerable flexibility in the future development of their specific configuration. Such a planning strategy makes it possible to establish, with a certain degree of flexibility, a relationship between fixed and dynamic values in order to guide the development process of the project matrix. Campagnola, constructed around a medieval castle, forms part of the conservation program of the vernacular environment, which also includes the village of Boccaleone and the buildings scattered along the old road that runs between them.

Superimposed on the territory is a matrix of "enveloping volumes," which relates one sector of the project to the other, measuring the volumetric quantities according to a helicoidal geometry in which diverse topological conditions interrelate in a continuum.

12. Project matrix for Bergamo city district.

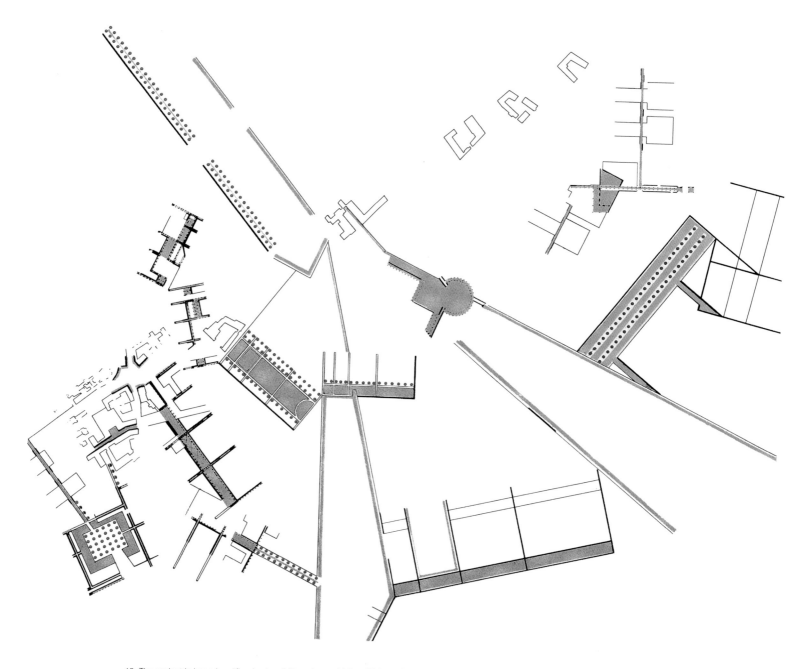

13. The project is based on "fixed values" (the urban voids) and "dynamic values" (the architectonic structures with considerable flexibility).

14–19. Views of model showing the spatial continuum of park and edifice.

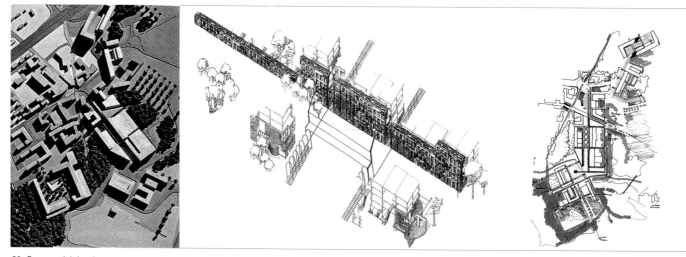

20. Commercial development structured by the street-gallery at Campagnola.

21. Residential development structured by pedestrian linear path leading into the new Campagnola Square.

This method gives rise to choices "through geometric interpolation," which besides ensuring a figurative continuum and homogeneous visual perception, resolve the often ambiguous relationship between the building development of the private sphere and the "urban voids" of the public sphere, between the dynamic and the fixed values.

The link between the project sector and the urban axis, Via Papa Giovanni XXIII, is the proposed railway overpass restricted to mass transportation: This will impede indiscriminate expansion into the plain, which is bounded by hills and populated areas such as Palazzo, Santa Caterina, Pignalo, and Sant'Alessandro. The distribution of the green areas, like a series of "climatic lungs," encourages pedestrian movement and drastically reduces rapid transit across the area. As far as the Morla Stream is concerned, the suggestion is to divert it into two basins on the southern slope that the future suburbs will overlook. The supplementary services of the existing settlements generate "circuits of involvement" and energetic "nodes of collision" through the intelligent juxtaposition of fragments integrated in an overall vital urban circuit.

This project is an intervention of powerful environmental unity, with the objective of bridging the gap between what Marshall McLuhan defines as "cool media" (in other words, commercial activities) and "hot media" (the humanity of the context, which houses 6,550 people between Boccaleone and Campagnola). This model of planning would arrest the outgoing demographic flux and oppose the current trend of unplanned fragmentation of the territory.

The hollowed-out square volume containing the museum, congress center, and theater auditorium is linked up via a filter of trees to the basic semistacked structures of the trade-fair complex, to be used for temporary and permanent expositions as well as special unconventional events. Following the same strategy, the design of the residential sectors makes the

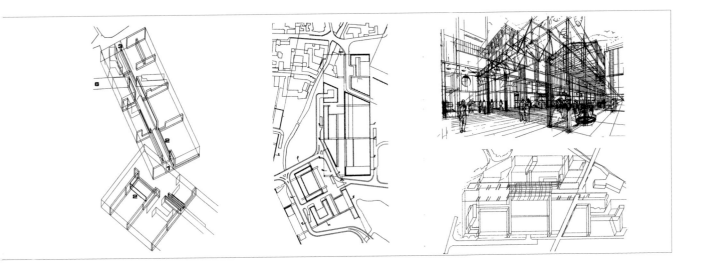

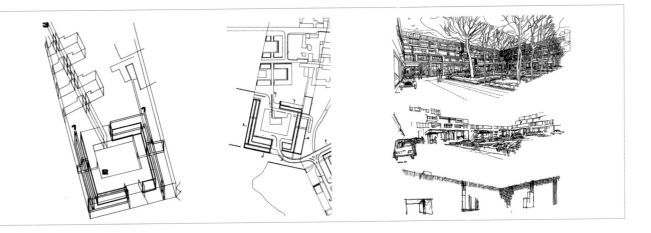

housing development gravitate on and around the public urban voids, expressed in the form of a lowered quadrangular piazza, a linear gallery, and a multifaceted sequence of spaces and routes that are all strictly interconnected with the pedestrian network of porticoes. The result is a large number of meeting places aimed at establishing "the space of interaction as a prototypical model of urban identity."

The architects add: "We are escaping from megalomaniac Utopia. Our country has no need of it. This is not an abstract proposal, but rather a realistic one that we have studied from all its finer administrative viewpoints, so that it will not be filed away in archives already full of so many lost opportunities. The proposal is all-inclusive. It is both rationally and economically viable and can therefore be transformed rapidly into an urban environment that people can use."

They therefore attach considerable importance to the discussion provoked by the exhibition: "The invitation to take part is serious. We urge not only the city administration but also private owners, businessmen, and citizens to take this risk with us. The same lots subject to expropriation can be converted into shares in the development of this city district." The Bergamo community will, however, have the last word.

Spatial Imagery

Park Avenue Apartment, New York

1

C. RAY SMITH
Avenue
December 1978

Piero Sartogo designs optical illusions. Sartogo pokes his face through one of the "invisible" doors in the spacious apartment and peers at a single tall white column in the living room. The column stands free in one corner, not quite touching the ceiling. It is not holding anything up, as columns are expected to do, but simply standing there.

When Sartogo closes the door, it does become invisible, blending perfectly with the walls and moldings around it. Not even a knob betrays its presence. "It's a psychological game, a perceptual thing," Sartogo explains of the room, as if he were in a scene from a Cocteau film.

To a degree, the Italian architect's work has a similar air of surrealism. Born and educated in Rome, where he practices and teaches architecture, Piero Sartogo spent a few early years as an architect in collaboration with Walter Gropius's Rome office of the Architects Collaborative, and for a decade was on the editorial board of the Italian architectural journal Casabella. He comes to teach in the United States every other year or so at a number of architecture schools, most recently at Columbia University.

"This is my first real work of interior architecture," he says of the apartment.

Most of his work is in urban planning — he has designed city centers for Bergamo and Karlsruhe and a housing project in Milan. In Milan he played something of a large-scale architectural device, or what he likes to call a "perceptual system." He ordered the buildings painted black on the upper stories and white on the lower stories, with a diagonal line separating the colors. The stripes across each building are aligned, so that when seen from afar the complex has a very powerful identity emerging from the landscape.

At the apartment, a system of stucco-like finished walls with traditional moldings contrasts with a system of floors, ceilings, and columns, like the overlaying in collages. "I work with collages," Sartogo admits, "the idea being that the environment

1. Placement of column at intersection of flooring grid.
2–4. The movement of the invisible door in the apartment.

2   3   4

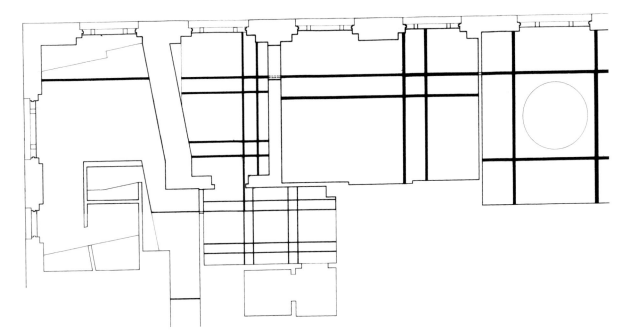

5. Inlaid aluminum strips in the gridded flooring get progressively wider from one room to the next.

is complex. It is an exaggeration of forms, and each of them is quite independent." American architects call it "layering." The owner, Sartogo says, may use virtually any style of furnishing he likes, and it will not be out of place. But the columns and floor design of the apartment function as sight gags.

The foyer floor consists of highly polished epoxy, in a purplish-red and black design, inlaid with aluminum strips that exactly reflect the pattern of the ceiling beams. Where the aluminum strips intersect, there are four white columns. They do not touch the ceiling either. In the library, which adjoins the foyer, there are more columns, but only two. Finally there is the living room, with its single white column. In each successive room, as the number of columns decreases, their size increases. "It's designed on a motif of spiral growth," Sartogo explains, by which the columns get larger and larger from room to room. Similarly, the inlaid aluminum strips in the gridded flooring get progressively wider from one room to the next and the next. It is analogous to the chambers of a nautilus, which grow progressively longer and wider as they spiral outward from the center of the shell.

We are to understand, Sartogo feels, that the rooms of the apartment grow in size and importance as one passes from the entrance to the principal living room. It is a literary idea, perhaps even metaphysical decorating. "I don't agree," Sartogo argues, "because decorating is to set up a stage condition in which everything is seen almost at once. Here there is constant reference to the third dimension because of the columns. They are a proportioning system for each space, establishing scale and points of reference and giving a three-dimensional reflection of the plan."

The plan is even more complicated than it appears. Each column is constructed of units — sections of column stacked on top of one another — and the smaller columns are constructed of more sections than the larger ones. Thus another hierarchy is apparent. The four columns in the foyer have four units each, the two in the middle room three, and the single column in the living room two. Furthermore, the individual column segments double in size from room to room.

"So they grow on the Golden Section," Sartogo explains, which is a proportioning system of classical architecture. "It is all a means of achieving psychological continuity between one space and the other," he says. "The physical reality of the space is irrelevant to the perceptual psychological reality.

"The systems of spiral growth and hierarchy make the individual spaces of the apartment seem continuous, flowing, processional.

6

7

6–8. The "march of columns" through the apartment begins in the entry hall, continues through the library, moves through the living room, and leads to the dining room. Designed by Giulio Paolini, the columns create an evocative sense of monumentality, often a component in Italian domestic design in the grand manner.

"I wanted to suggest that space itself is a sort of psychological game," Sartogo says. "I have been accused in Italy of being a painter who does architecture. Most modern architecture is independent from its context, its surroundings. So buildings are self-contained objects, self-explanatory, self everything. They don't produce any meanings.

"I think Claes Oldenburg made that irony of modern architecture so clear. I am interested in the relationship between the object and the context. To define the context there is the functional aspect, but perceptual aspects are also very relevant to formal aspects, because without them there is no function. One of the most relevant layers of the environment is the sense, the psychology, the quality of space — more than just the physical, volumetric layout."

What Sartogo seems to be saying is that the complexity of life requires complex responses and, in the case of his design for this New York apartment, complex environments.

8

"All my work is to search for codes," he says. "Language, expression, semantics, meanings in architecture. It is like saying the linguistic manifestation of architecture is the interplay between the systems. The expression of architecture, as far as I am concerned, comes out of the placement of an ordering structure and the contextual intrusion or incidence that sets a thing in a particular condition or on a particular site. Linguistic expression is in the tension between the two."

There is another identity to the apartment, one that comes from Sartogo's feeling for materials, from his interesting harsh rich walls — "walls that feel like they are breathing" — and from the Paolini columns and grids and moldings that fill the public rooms. The aura the apartment has, finally, is that of classicism. It is startlingly modern, but one feels the sensibility of a classical Italian palazzo informing and stimulating all of the architect's ideas. A feeling of classicism in the midst of experimentation is perhaps the finest quality — and the most subtle of all the contradictions Piero Sartogo has chosen to explore.

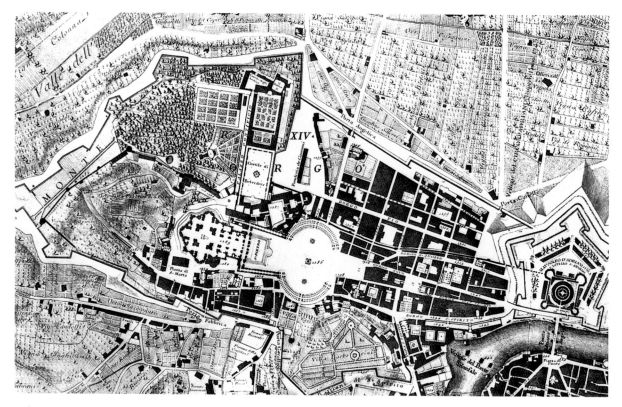

1. Gian Battista Nolli's plan of Rome, 1747, sector 1, which includes Hadrian's mausoleum (Castel Sant'Angelo), the Borgo (before its partial demolition by Mussolini), and the Vatican.

2. "Roma Interrotta," 1978, sector 1, showing how Rome might have developed under a radical secular spirit informed by the utopian theories of Charles Fourier.

3

Roma Interrotta

City-Planning Project and Exhibition

The exhibition "Rome Interrotta" held at Trajan's Market poses three questions: Is the idea valid or, at least, sensible? Are the architects who have been asked to participate in it sufficiently representative? Does the result serve any purpose in cultural terms? The answers are: yes, no, and maybe.

BRUNO ZEVI
Cronache di Architettura
1978

Let us first look at what this unusual undertaking consists of. In 1748, the engraver Gian Battista Nolli produced a splendid plan of Rome that represents the last document of coherent urban "design" for the city. The current exhibition proposal was made to entrust its 12 compartments to contemporary architects of various nationalities with this premise: Cancel all that has happened in 230 years of inertia and land speculation, and redesign Rome as you would like, starting from Nolli. An odd project but undoubtedly stimulating for a city that since the 19th century has lost all sense of planned development.

It was necessary to select an array of brilliant and heretical names, of opposing tendencies. But in the list made up of Costantino Dardi, Romaldo Giurgola, Michael Graves, Antoine Grumbach, Leon and Robert Krier, Paolo Portoghesi, Aldo Rossi, Colin Rowe, Piero Sartogo, James Stirling, and Robert Venturi, there is a clear prevalence of classicist, baroque, and neo-Islamic "historicists" who aggravate the Italian disease of rhetoric. With all the difficulties Rome has had to face in the past, at least it has been spared the misdeeds of these latter.

We can identify seven imaginative trends in the 12 projects: 1) the pseudo-Piranesi visions; 2) the De Chirico revivals; 3) the myth of the *genius loci;* 4) the professional approach; 5) the pop-art mask. What remain are two of the most brilliant and courageous projects of all, the only ones that have captured the provocative thrust of the theme and confronted it without cerebral distortion or agnosticism: 6) Stirling's masterly "collage." The architecture is his, embodied in the "pieces" that have made him famous: the St. Andrew's student dormitories, the Cambridge library, the segmented complex in Oxford, and the grid plan of Runcorn. These design elements are played with and astutely distributed in Nolli's plan. 7) The courageous heretical direction taken by Sartogo. Especially because of its application to the nucleus of the Vatican neighborhood, it is extremely effective. It proposes the only plausible turn for the growth of Rome by concentrating on the issues. In 1748, according to Sartogo's plan, the Pope decided to emigrate to South America and left all ecclesiastical property to the future "social departments" (the so-called phalansteries of sociologist Charles Fourier, 1772–1837). It was therefore possible to create "Fourierist harmony in the northwest sector, in the area comprising Hadrian's mausoleum (Castel Sant'Angelo) and the Valley of the Inferno and the furnaces (the former name of the Vatican City)."

The dialogue between the new fabric and the context is rationally resolved by making space via subtraction from the solid mass of the urban fabric, by opening up the street. Now the urban organism has finally developed a backbone, overcoming the opposition between poetry and prose, monuments and ordinary buildings, closed static spaces and itineraries. Secular culture now dominates and this is indispensable for any authentic change to Rome's urban character.

3. The original 1748 Gian Battista Nolli plan of Rome consists of 12 engraved plates.

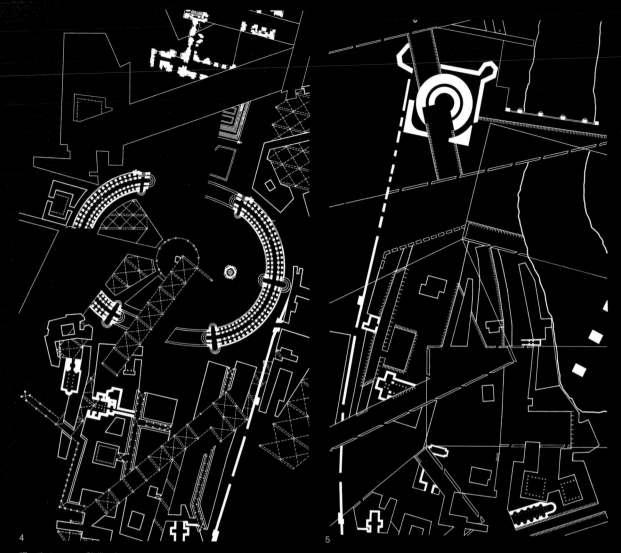

4   5

"For those many Civilized persons who wish to know how they should act in their own interests in order to make the best use of the residue of civilization, the following is the best advice I can give them: 'Do not undertake any new building. The arrangement of civilized buildings is incompatible with the practices of the New Order. It will be necessary to carry out radical modifications of all your houses if they are to be of any use. Even so, a great number of them will remain unusable. Let not the owners take alarm at this, however, since the global hierarchy will indemnify them for any damages which arise from the establishment of the New Order.'" —Charles Fourier

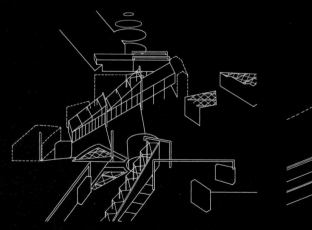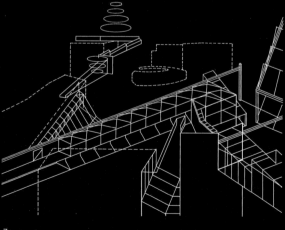

6   7

4–7. The primary objective of the Vatican zone (plan, fig. 4, and three-dimensional scheme, fig. 6) and the Borgo zone (figs. 5 and 7) is to transform a static urban fabric into a dynamic one. In part this is accomplished through internal and street galleries that form an enclosed and continuous system in the urban fabric.

The deepest cut of all must certainly be irony. With Sartogo and Leon Krier, Lissitzky's red wedge twice penetrates the white citadel of religion and rhetoric, casting doubt on Bernini's ecumenical embrace. That old mole (Fourier before Marx) is not only a subterranean ghost but a bulldozer that acts in the light of day, shattering antiquated history: Sartogo's scissors cut up the paper tiger that is the Vatican, wielding political irony to exorcise the memory of the redemptive pickax. In the vast theater of Renaissance-Baroque Rome, this *danse macabre* ends in a sort of social idyll and the volume of St. Peter's becomes the Rome Opera House and the venue of ballet.

Historical analysis uncovers the most recondite folds of the anatomy of Rome. But is this a matter of vivisection or of autopsy? "Utopia," writes Carlo Argan, "is the atheistic opposite of providence: Imagination is the providence of the nonreligious, and Rome, we hope, will finally be secular or it will cease to exist." Will our imagination overcome the difficulties of Weimar and ascend to power? Or will our city have to content itself with a paper triumph? For the moment there is inevitably far too much ideology both in the consecration of history (as an orgiastic din of a museum or a silent museum) and in its epitaph. The shadow of the Plan Voisin can only lead to the plan as the cemetery of history and of its forms.

MARCELLO FAGIOLO
DELL'ARCO
Modo
October 1979

8–9. These images, read from top to bottom, illustrate the imagined interventions in and around St. Peter's Square, Rome.

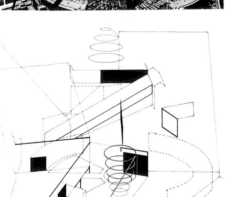
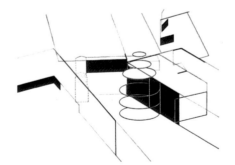

8

9

Living Space in Counterpoint

1

RUDOLF ARNHEIM
Unpublished essay
1982

Architecture is experienced through all the senses, with the probable exception of taste. One can have a taste for architecture but one is not likely to practice it with the tongue. Neither smell nor the sense of temperature are excluded from architectural experience. For the purpose of practical analysis, however, one distinguishes the world of tangible objects, as perceived by the sense of touch and the kinesthetic experiences that report on the body's movement through space, from the visual images received by the eyes. I will speak of the physical as against the visual world, although this terminology is by no means tidy, either psychologically or epistemologically. Strictly speaking, the "physical" world, being a world of experience, is no more physical than the visual world. It is purely perceptual; and it does not exclude vision because the eyes report as much about the nature of physical objects as do touch and the muscle sense.

In architectural practice, however, it is convenient to distinguish between things as they are and things as they look. The architectural "program," as worked out with the client, refers mainly to the physical objects to be built. In creating his design, the architect also gives much thought to appearance. In good architecture the two aspects are not considered separately. The way in which they are related, however, varies depending on style.

To the eyes of the viewer, much traditional architecture integrates the two approaches so thoroughly that it seems artificial to consider them separately. What we see when we look at the Parthenon is born out essentially by what is ascertained by touch and measurement. To be sure, the eyes receive a different image depending on where the viewer is standing at a given time. But this difference is mostly one of optical projection. What is actually perceived is the one invariable object. This stability of the object is due not only to what psychologists know as the constancy of size and shape, namely the compensation of the projective distortions. In addition, there is what one should call "the constancy of the object." Regardless of the point of observation, the viewer sees the same object, as long as certain conditions are met. The Parthenon is the Parthenon, from wherever we look at it.

The so-called architectural refinements of ancient buildings do not contradict this observation but confirm it. The slight deviations from the straight line and the right angle are not introduced to create a difference between what is seen and what is physically there. On the contrary, they are meant to make us see what is actually there. According to the usual explanation, they are intended as corrections of perceptual deformations that would keep us from seeing the intended cubic shape. There is no perceivable discrepancy between what the building is and what it looks like.

1. Untitled collage (1971) by Piero Sartogo.

The refinements of the Greek temples also have been interpreted as a means of counteracting the rigidity of straightness and rectangularity. The slight swelling of the columns, for example, enhances their visual dynamics. Such dynamic qualities are an addition to the buildings as "physical" objects. But they are intended to enhance the character of what the building is, not to create a perceivable difference between what it is and what it looks like.

Unless I am mistaken, a distinct deviation from this integrated unity between being and appearance occurs only in Baroque architecture. The illusory spaces of Bernini's Scala Regia in the Vatican or Borromini's colonnade in the garden of the Palazzo Spada cannot have been expected to remain undetected by the viewers (fig. 2). They were intended to demonstrate playfully that there exists a duality between the way things are and the way they are seen. The philosophical conclusion suggested by those magic tricks was not that our world is nothing but a misleading illusion. It proposes a more interesting complication of the world view by asserting that reality consists of an interplay between the way things are and the way they appear.

It seems to me that this conception is the underlying theme of Piero Sartogo's architectural designs. I would be unwilling to call his inventions "surrealistic." Surrealism aims at presenting an absurd world as an image of the world's absurdity. Sartogo indulges in such an attitude only with an occasional detail, as for example when in the entrance hall of the Ginori Store in Rome he parodies the pretentious stone columns of a bourgeois palazzo's façade with truncated rubber columns loosely placed on a polished floor of black marble (figs. 3–4). Magritte and Duchamp would approve of such a paradox, and the architect himself smiles at the sight. But more often he is quite serious even when he plays, because by playing he explores the conditions of the human experience.

2. Borromini's colonnade, Palazzo Spada, Rome.

3. At the Richard Ginori showroom in Via del Tritone, Rome, the scale of existing façade is projected into recessed atrium.

4. New rubber columns structure the entry into the central gallery of the Ginori showroom.

I cannot think of examples to fill the historical gap between the baroque approach I mentioned and Sartogo's concern with similar problems. But it would not be difficult to find such effects here and there in the designs of other architects today, even though nobody else seems to have devoted himself to them with such concentration. They are architectural experiments, pointing to questions that have haunted the philosophical imagination of our time.

A most striking case in point is Sartogo's design for the Gescal housing project in Milan (figs. 11–14). As physical objects, the nine groups of three apartment towers have the monotony to which architects conform, especially when they have to meet the specifications of government authorities. But a dimension of freedom offered itself in the visual surface structure of the high-rise cubes. By subdividing the outer walls into an upper area of dark color and a lower area of white, the architect obtained a twofold enrichment. He added to the uniformity of the physical shape the kind of pattern that one might compare to the decorations often used in ceramics. On archaic Greek vases, for example, bands of various designs subdivide the sculptural shape of the vessel. In addition, the color pattern on the buildings strengthened the distinction between the different aspects obtained when the housing project is viewed from different points of observation.

The nine groups of cubic towers, taken as mere shapes, present of course different perspective views depending on where one stands. But without further assistance, this variety would offer only slight visual stimulation. The different vistas would have no memorable individuality and would add up therefore to nothing more than a combinatory play. They would not disagree with the statement that no matter from where one looked one was confronted with the same invariable array of volumes.

This impression would not be substantially altered if the subdivision by color created a horizontal boundary at a uniform level. It would create a stable and immobile distinction between an upper dark world and a lower bright one. Such an effect can be desirable for certain purposes, as Sartogo himself has shown when he wrapped broad bands of dark ribbon around the columns of the Palazzo delle Esposizioni in Rome, thereby lowering the central hall to the human level as the setting for an art exhibition (figs. 5–10). This horizontal splicing of the space was strengthened by the contrast between lighting at the ground level and darkness in the cupola. (At the same time, the large space of the dome above remained dimly visible — a solution characteristic of Sartogo, who, as we shall see, likes to show contradictory aspects simultaneously rather than offering either/or decisions.)

5–8. "Vitalità del negativo" at the Palazzo delle Esposizioni in Rome. Central hall before staging of exhibition (fig. 5). Measuring the dimensions of the new volume (fig. 6). A section sign divides above from below, dark from light (fig. 7). Wrapping broad bands of dark ribbon around the columns (fig. 8).

9. In the Palazzo delle Esposizioni, the neoclassical dome is obscured by the positioning of the projectors. The projected visitor's shadows are in scale with the huge bases of the 20 nodal columns.

10. The architectural framework designed to connect the giant columns in the central hall.

11. Model of project matrix for Gescal Public Housing Development in Milan.

Horizontal slicing of this kind is not used for the color scheme of the Gescal towers because it would emphasize the monotony of the project. Instead the contours between dark and white run obliquely across the walls and change direction at the corners. This gives each of the four walls a characteristic face of its own.

In addition to considering the appearance of each building, however, Sartogo is very interested in the interrelation between the groups of towers. This interrelation is hardly activated by the physical volumes of the buildings. Their identical shape and the parallelism of their vertical and horizontal orientation in space indicate their kinship; but mere similarity is a weak kind of relation. It says nothing better than: "We are all the same, and therefore we belong together." Such a distressing message of monotony Sartogo wished to counteract. He attempted to do it by establishing visual connections between the color areas of adjoining buildings.

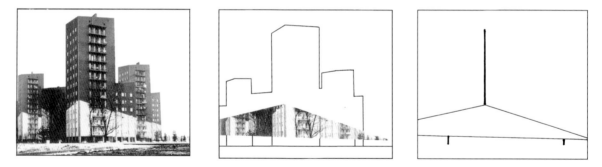

12. The counterpoint between physical and visual reality at Gescal.

In the extreme case, the contour between dark and white leaps in visual continuity from building to building (figs. 11–12). Seen by itself, this view tends to create the illusion of a transparent curtain or veil — a fascinating effect, which, however, has the architectural disadvantage of splitting the image into two independent components. One tends to see the curtain in front and the building behind it, without much of the unity that is needed for every successful design. To illustrate the effect, I may be permitted to refer here to an experiment that the Gestalt psychologist Max Wertheimer sometimes demonstrated in his classes at the New School for Social Research in New York and that, if I remember correctly, has never been described. On a turntable he piled a disorderly heap of boxes and other objects. In the darkened classroom he projected the slide of some picture or photograph upon this arrangement. As long as there was not movement, the projected image was seen as broken up into cubistically disconnected facets. But when the turntable was put into slow motion, the image detached itself from the vehicle and was seen as standing in midair, in front of the rotating display, as though projected on a nonexistent screen. The optically given disorderly situation had split up into two separate percepts.

Such a split comes about when the perceptual situation can be "improved" by creating two structurally simpler patterns. It is likely to occur in the particular case of Sartogo's Gescal project when the contour of the coloring continues across the spatial distance between building and building. This creates an illusion that interferes with the architect's intention, because it

13. The difference between real and virtual, here seen from the highway, can only be experienced by visiting the complex.

14. View from the park.

detaches the visual curtain from the buildings instead of showing the interplay between the two components. Sartogo is rarely interested in illusions; he wants to demonstrate the counterpoint between physical and visual reality. To this end, the physical and the visual components have to be equally real, and they must appear as indivisibly connected.

The illusion occurs, however, only in the particular views for which the contours are continuous. This is not the case in the many other views, and while our illustrations of the architectural sights cannot but single out an isolated particular vista, the actual experience intended by the architect comes about as a movement in time. Driving or walking around or through the housing complex, one perceives a continuous change of aspects (figs. 13–14). All of them are inseparably related by the context of the temporal sequence; and in this context, physical shape and color pattern are intimately connected.

The connection is of a very particular nature. In new and old architecture, walls have sometimes been animated by different coloring. But in practically all instances, the color pattern conforms to the relief structure of the wall. In the simplest case, the trim of the windows is set off against the masonry; or the rhythm of window rows or pilasters is supported by vertical or horizontal bands of color. In keeping with the tradition, the physical and the visual aspects of the building remain fused. Sartogo's contours, however, cut boldly across the physical structure and thereby make it quite clear that the coloring is to be perceived as a separate system. In musical terms, one might say that instead of aiming at harmonic fusion, the architect presents a counterpoint between two separate parts. Counterpoint is defined in the dictionary as "the musical technique of combining two or more melodic lines in such a way that they establish a harmonic relationship while retaining their linear individuality." This is precisely the formula applied by Piero Sartogo again and again in his designs.

The effect created by this device amounts, as I said earlier, to more than visual stimulation. It endows each aspect of each building and of the total group of buildings with its own visual individuality and thereby points to the possibility of overcoming the anonymity of the single person or group in a mass society. What is more, the coloring overrules the distressing separateness of the towers. It creates connections between them by providing a variety of parallels and opposites, continuations and breaks, which play across the total panorama. This visual display of contrapuntal effects suggests symbolically that there exist active relations between the various living units, that these relations are endlessly variable, and that they are not obtained in easy harmony with the structure of each unit but at the price of an almost violent tension — the tension, namely, between the design of the cubic building and the design of the color pattern. If the viewer's mind is ready for the perception of such a sight and its implications, he will understand it as the visual announcement of a challenging social task, deriving from the living together of hundreds of families.

I have discussed the Gescal design in some detail because it seems to me to illustrate the theme that underlies Sartogo's architectural thinking. But there are other ways of exploring the interplay of contrapuntal experiences, and they, too, are exemplified in Sartogo's work. Consider the relations between physical separation and visual connection. Architecture, one might say, consists always of a set of partitions, which act as constraints upon the coming and going of people. They separate them from another, they fence them in, they define their territories, they channel their paths. In each case, the physical partition involves the choice of one place to the exclusion of all others. This limitation makes for a one-sided way of life unless it is counteracted by its opposite, i.e., by connection.

16. The positioning of the nets in gradually increasing numbers creates a more and more solid volume as the exhibit route progresses.

15. The Villa Borghese underground parking garage before the Contemporanea exhibition in Rome.

Partitions, although physically impenetrable to anybody but a violent transgressor, can be visually penetrable to varying degrees. At one extreme there is the totally opaque wall, which confirms the obstacle faced by the body. A first measure of penetration is offered by translucency, exemplified by our modern glass blocks or the alabaster windows of ancient churches. It announces the presence of light in a world beyond the partition and lets that vital energy enter the room. It counteracts the experience of being enclosed, but it does so in the most rarefied way possible. Only the transparency of glass and similar materials lets the existence of the outer world become more explicit. Through a window we see that outer world in all its concreteness. But there is a distinct contradiction between the visual availability of that other world and the impossibility of our stepping into it physically. The poignant tension between the two versions of our relations to the next world becomes even more marked when no windowpane holds us back and instead there is an actual opening. In modern apartments or offices — and Sartogo has an example of it in his Roman apartment — separate living or work spaces are often openly accessible to one another, yet their separateness is to be respected. A corridor leads from the bedroom to the dining room; it invites passage, but the distinctness of the two rooms' functions imposes a constraint on easy intercourse.

Varying degrees of transparency can express corresponding degrees of separation. In the Contemporanea exhibition, organized in a subterranean parking garage in Rome (fig. 15), different sections were assigned to the visual, literary, and performing arts. It wa*s desirable to show that each artistic activity is autonomous but also belongs to the family of the arts (fig. 18). Sartogo conveyed this thought by using wire netting for partitions (fig. 16). This material provided semi-transparent walls, displaying the counterpoint of unity versus diversity. At the same time the light was filtered through more than one partition so that for each viewing point the transparency differed in density, indicating different degrees of connection and isolation. The invitation to override the partitions was conveyed by a bright beam of neon tubing that ran unimpeded across the ceiling of the entire exhibition area (fig.17).

There are other ways of overcoming partitions, more sophisticated because they require that the viewer's perceptions go beyond what can be directly seen. Take the simple example of a line traced on the floor to meet an opaque wall and continuing on the other side. Unless the partition is freestanding, one cannot see both sections of the line as parts of the same image. But human perception is not limited to relations that can be observed in simultaneity. It constantly supplements what is given — in the simplest case, when we see an object as an all-around volume although only its frontal aspect can be perceived at any one moment. A mind-stretching experience is provided by that line on the floor, which invites us to enlarge our perception to include the space on the other side of the partition.

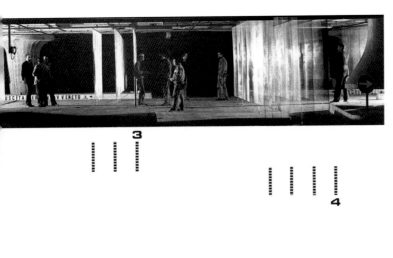

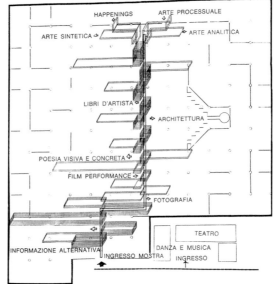

17. The layout of the nets creates a kind of conceptual diaphragm, an apparent mass of solid volume that is penetrable. This image tends to annul the effect of "the beginning and the end" of the exhibition route, making each sector an autonomous entity.

18. Plan of the exhibit.

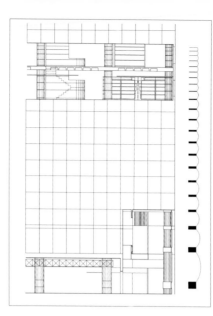

19. The Italian Trade Center, New York. The vertical progression through the floors, from the cellar level to the sixth level, creates the building's new time-space sequence.

Partitions can be counteracted in this fashion not only in the horizontal direction but also in the vertical. This imposes an even more demanding task on the viewer. The horizontal plane, being the dimension of action, suggests perceptual cross-connections between neighboring spaces, but we have little practice in acknowledging similar relations in the vertical. Staircases and elevators pierce the horizontal planes, thereby violating the planes' perceptual integrity. Sartogo undertook to interconnect the four floors of a New York building that were designed to house the Italian Trade Center.

Such a visual integration was all the more desirable since the four floors were not contiguous. The lower floors, devoted mainly to display and contact with the public, were detached from the more administrative functions of the offices on the fifth and sixth floors of the building. "A vertical progression of horizontal bands on columns and other elements begins at the cellar level and accelerates to the sixth floor. The width of the bands and the spaces between them decreases as the bands ascend" (fig. 19).

Here the designer has shrewdly taken advantage of the psychological difference between a constant beat and an accelerating gradient. A constant rhythm has no beginning and no end. A column decorated with bands of equal width and intervals would willingly stop at the floor and the ceiling and would not suggest any piercing of the horizontal partitions; whereas a gradient is possessed by directed dynamics. A gradient is an arrow, pointing forward and displaying the will to penetrate all obstacles. As a means of establishing a vertical connection it is not only effective but also particularly appropriate, since an ascent from below is experienced as an increasing effort to overcome the pull of gravity.

Tracings on the floor and ceiling and on the walls can fulfill other significant functions. I mentioned earlier the visual enrichment of volumes by means of painted subdivisions. In addition to the external skin of volumes, architecture deals with interior surfaces, which fulfill very different functions, and with what may be called "connecting spaces." Connecting spaces bridge the gaps between volumes and assume tangible shape in such surfaces as streets and floors. As I have shown in a book of mine on architecture, the hollows or "negative spaces" assume a positive function by serving as channels for the coming and going of users. The hollow canyon of the street is converted from "ground" into "figure," to use psychological language. This positive function of the channels of human traffic is emphasized perceptually by markings such as sidewalks, dividing lines, etc. On the floors of interiors, lines and contours along corridors show the way and encourage movement.

Less obvious is the use of demarcations between living spaces by means of different colors and textures. Such divisions erect invisible walls between spaces that are physically contiguous. Psychologists are well acquainted with shapes that are perceptually real although not presented by any stimulation of the eyes' retinas. A drawing of a cube, for example, that offers retinally nothing but the contour lines, produces an image of the cube's side walls, which are perceptually quite real although not actually represented in the drawing.

In the same way, one can erect in a hollow space virtual walls or volumes that are produced perceptually by mere induction through contours or single side-faces. Once again a characteristic counterpoint is obtained between partitions or volumes not constructed physically but quite real visually (fig. 20). Of particular interest are the tracings of corners, which make it possible for us to see the inside and the outside of partial cubes at the same time as though we were able to resort to a fourth dimension of space.

In addition, it is possible for the designer to overcome the dichotomy between filled and empty spaces and to give tangible appearance to the fields of forces that are created for the eye in the environment surrounding architectural objects. For example, two pillars standing at a short distance from each other will animate the space between them, which can be made explicit by a band of color or texture on the floor. The power of volumes to fill the spatial intervals with reverberations of their own structure was studied in the paintings of certain Cubist artists, such as Lyonel Feininger. In Sartogo's Roman apartment, markings of contours on floor, walls, and ceilings populate the hollows of the interior with partitions and volumes that are not there physically.

20. The volumetric reality of the Rome Apartment is modified by virtual volumes.

One further perceptual feature I would like to discuss is Sartogo's frequent use of gradients. A visual gradient is a continuous change of size, intervals, brightness, color, etc. Most often it comes about optically as an effect of projection: With increasing distance from the eyes, objects become smaller, distances narrower, colors dimmer. Of course, these phenomena are not found objectively in the physical environment. Therefore they attract the attention of anybody who is fascinated by the interplay of physical space and visual appearance.

The converging lines of edges of central perspective correspond physically to parallels. Therefore, to introduce such sheaves of vectors into the actual design amounts to teasingly intermingling the domains of projective appearance and physical existence. In the Roman apartment, Sartogo has such a sheaf of diverging lines and bands issue from the inside of the entrance door and spread through the adjoining rooms (figs. 21–22).

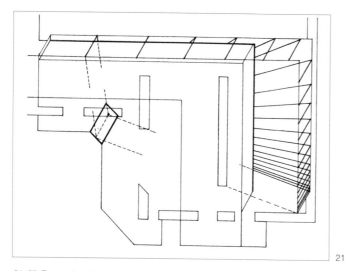

21–22. Focused on the entry door, the incremental gradient occupies the space generating the directed dynamics on the perimeter. The Rome apartment's perspective lines are inlaid in ceiling and wall.

22

Such a device, if successful, offers a counterpoint between the coordination of juxtaposed cubic spaces and a hierarchy focused in a center and expanding from there to ever-growing distances. It opposes the reversibility of the relation among spaces, by which it makes little difference in which direction the occupant is walking or looking. Instead there is a crescendo of enlarging space if one proceeds from the center or decrescendo in the inverse direction.

In the corridor of the Ginori Store, brightness gradients of various colors merge smoothly with the gradients of foreshortened sizes and distances introduced by optical projections. These sequences of vertical colored stripes not only strengthen the depth effect of the passageway but also enrich the objective monotony of the elongated opening by a dynamic progress, which is experienced by visitors as they walk from the entrance of the store to the showrooms.

In all the projects here discussed, a formal pattern was designed for a physical array of volumes and open spaces. The pattern is not simply imposed upon the given situation but also found in it. In fact, the success of the design depends on the appropriateness of the invention for the architectural purpose. An extreme example of this relationship presents itself when the plan of a whole city, which has come about typically as a mixture of intentional organization and accidental accretion, is fitted to a simple geometrical shape. For the purpose of urban renewal in the city of Bergamo, Sartogo has proposed the figure of a spiral, which is suggested, he finds, by significant buildings and spaces of the existing cityscape and suitable as a guiding pattern for changes and additions (figs. 23–25).

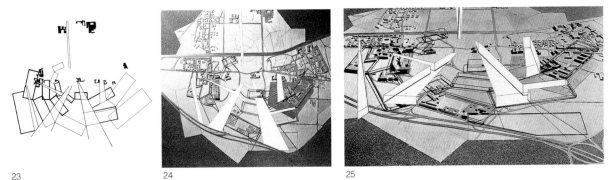

23 24 25

23–25. Deriving from a perceptual analysis of the context, the matrix of the Bergamo city district project outlines a system with a gradual helicoidal growth determining the "continuum" of the park and building of the urban plan.

The value of such a proposal depends, of course, on its suitability. But in principle no objectionable violence is perpetuated by such a procedure. In fact, it conforms to the nature of perception quite in general. Perception, we have come to understand, does not consist in the passive acceptance of external facts. It consists in finding form in the messages arriving from the outer world. Since those messages are by no means without form of their own, the perception will be appropriate only if the forms it puts forth do justice to the forms it finds. The artist and the scientist, at their own levels of operation, proceed similarly. They, too, deal with the world by giving it shape, but they, too, face the obligation of making their shapes do justice to those they reflect.

It seems characteristic of Piero Sartogo's particular approach to his work that in his case the function of the architect cannot be as neatly distinguished from that of the interior designer as is commonly possible. As a rule, the designer can be said to fill in where the architect has left off. He is given spaces to which he applies the shapes that make them livable. Sartogo, also, in most of the projects here described, uses a given setting — the Italian word is *ordito* — to invent a design appropriate for its use. Typically, however, he does not leave those given settings alone but modifies their very nature for the intended purpose, that is, he approaches them as an architect. The fruitfulness of this interaction, it seems to me, accounts for the originality of the solutions illustrated in the present book.

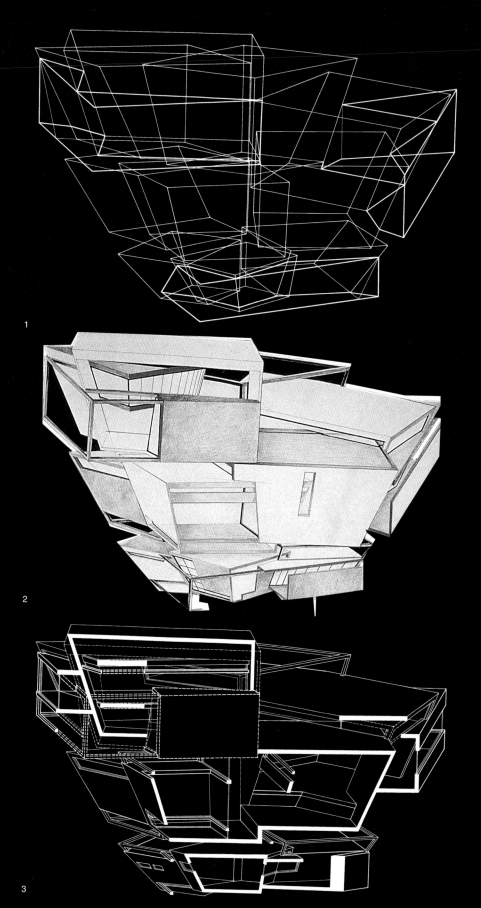

1–4. This design research project juxtaposes the real *ordito* and its virtual counterpart. Illustrations start with the spatial frame (fig. 1), develop its external volumetric configuration (fig. 2), and investigate in detail the interior-exterior space relations (fig. 3). A model represents the physical architectonic configuration (fig. 4).

The Virtual Method

4

From the images of architecture to the architecture of images.

If the enormous production of objects classified as architecture, being enlargements of preconceived forms (macrodesign), are excluded, architectural design exists solely and exclusively when the Platonic plan, the ideal model, the archetype, takes shape in a "unicum" through its dislocation in a particular context because of procedures such as distortion, alteration, and modification.

PIERO SARTOGO
Monograph published
by Centro di Firenze
1977

In the case of architecture for reality, the perceiver is obliged to receive information emanating from the image. But it seems that there is also architecture — virtual architecture — in which the subject becomes the element forming the image, in other words, the work of architecture itself.

There is then the problem of understanding the limits that distinguish architecture as an object from architecture as a subject, the real image from the virtual image. In designing an actual work of architecture, history and tradition have accustomed us to "see." But in design through "virtuality," we can attempt to "invent." Whenever in the history of modern architecture such attempts have actually been made, the great cloak of formal illusion has covered them so as to avoid the birth of an expressive antagonism that is unwelcome and eventually rejected. Adolf Loos and his struggle against ornament is one example. This freezing of the expressive idiom, from signs to paradigms reduced to the most basic elements, gave rise to "programmed" architecture, urbanistic and architectonic rationalism, the interchangeable and replaceable object, and the Bauhaus at its peak. After this came the "monument" of modern architecture. Despite this, other operations, because they were contradictory, ambiguous, and at times overambitious, generated a schismatic movement that never became orthodox.

This is a stream of thought that inevitably appears discontinuous, fragmentary, and never totally explicit, but one that nonetheless reappears at times of renewal during the crisis of the systematic formulations of the modern movement. This involves operations that range from the ambiguity of scale produced by a deformation of dimensions to the variations in context, from superimposition and juxtaposition and the matching and transparency of independent systems to bricolage, etc., etc. As I have already stated, there is no such thing as architecture without context, whether man-made or natural. In the city, for example, the element correlating urban and architectonic design is not always evident unless it is first expressed through the filter of perception specifically, subject by subject.

The same problem arises in the relationship between the outer and inner space of a building, often with resulting contra-

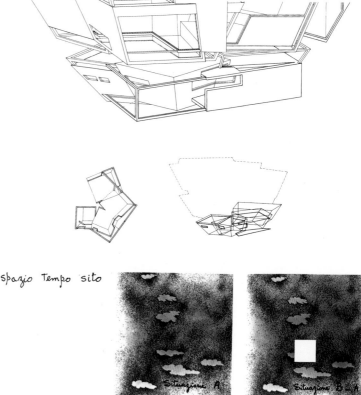

spazio Tempo sito

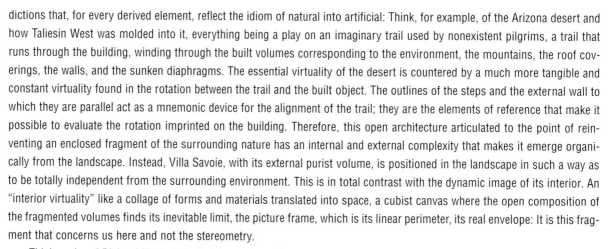

5

dictions that, for every derived element, reflect the idiom of natural into artificial: Think, for example, of the Arizona desert and how Taliesin West was molded into it, everything being a play on an imaginary trail used by nonexistent pilgrims, a trail that runs through the building, winding through the built volumes corresponding to the environment, the mountains, the roof coverings, the walls, and the sunken diaphragms. The essential virtuality of the desert is countered by a much more tangible and constant virtuality found in the rotation between the trail and the built object. The outlines of the steps and the external wall to which they are parallel act as a mnemonic device for the alignment of the trail; they are the elements of reference that make it possible to evaluate the rotation imprinted on the building. Therefore, this open architecture articulated to the point of reinventing an enclosed fragment of the surrounding nature has an internal and external complexity that makes it emerge organically from the landscape. Instead, Villa Savoie, with its external purist volume, is positioned in the landscape in such a way as to be totally independent from the surrounding environment. This is in total contrast with the dynamic image of its interior. An "interior virtuality" like a collage of forms and materials translated into space, a cubist canvas where the open composition of the fragmented volumes finds its inevitable limit, the picture frame, which is its linear perimeter, its real envelope: It is this fragment that concerns us here and not the stereometry.

Think again, of Richard Neutra's typical house, its real air-conditioned interior and its exterior, which consumes the landscape in a virtual mimesis achieved through opulent transparency. Both have a certain portion of virtuality, but to neither can we attribute that perception with which the image becomes fully virtual.

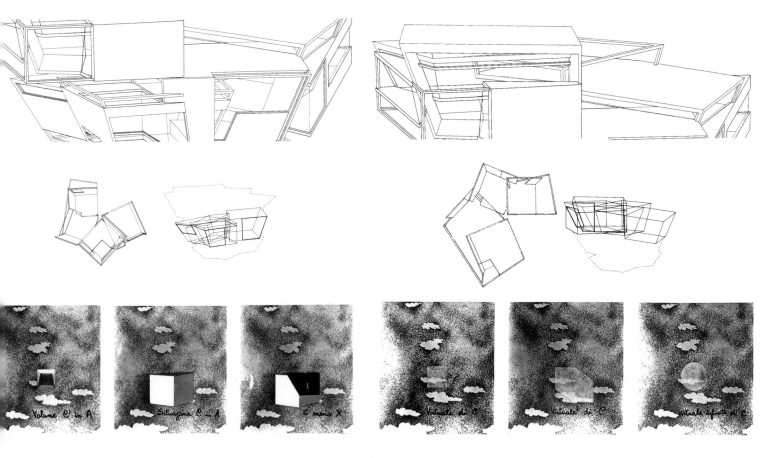

6   7

5–7. The development of individual parts of the design research project's revolving spiral organism, starting with its bottom and progressing upward.

The secret message, however, has been received by the visual operators, by all those who have made the virtual into a design strategy. From the great ironic monuments of Oldenburg to the kinetic art of Vasarely, not to mention Balla's objects, a system and method have begun to develop. It is worth remembering that there will come a day when, side by side with the real image of a magnifying and magnified architecture, we shall perhaps see a much more critical, liberating, ironic, and demythologizing architecture that, owing to these qualities, will perhaps be much more alive.

If two levels of relationship can be identified in architecture — the first, very real and concrete, which the individual acknowledges through his senses, and the second, at an abstract and conceptual level inherent in the object itself — it is possible to assume the simultaneous presence of both levels and the transfer from one to the other.

If we can assume this, it is the subject who establishes an architectural condition and dimension in a spatial environment. If the cognitive process of thinking is not independent from the process of perceiving, but rather an essential ingredient of perception itself, the result is that the "percept" is "concept." Architecture, being a visual language, records both levels of acknowledgement, visible and invisible, in its percept.

If the notion of space can be verified in either a solid volume or an open or closed void, and becomes significant through a sign, the result is that the design method is defined by the juxtaposition, either by matching or by transparency, between a real *ordito* and its virtual counterpart.

Piero Sartogo at the National Institute of Architecture

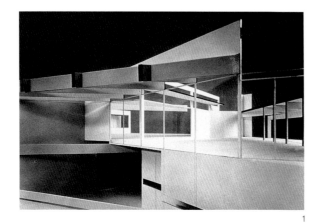

1

UMBERTO MICHELE
Finalità dell'Architettura
1977

Piero Sartogo's work springs from his perception that there is a contradiction between creating architecture and the secret fear that it is impossible to create architecture. The Inarch exhibition of April 18, 1977, is evidence of this perception: the extreme contradiction between an architecture that has to take account of the force of gravity, on the one hand, and of the possibility of utilizing space that is physical and psychological, on the other. The exhibit is presented through an idiom that is not the hobbled language of architects but the quest for an idiom through which the most recent experiments of the visual arts have passed. This indicates that readapting a field of relations and communications could offer architecture another possibility of manifesting its presence.

In one of his latest works, the Gescal Housing Development in Milan, one thing is clear: his refusal to remain silent. When the standards and architectonic typology are fixed, the problem is by no means solved; the composition is more for electronic brains than for architects. And the nondescript undifferentiated sameness of homes is the final operation of a pigeon-holing of minds in a logic that prefers not to make people think, but to offer pseudo-solutions. Indeed, the architect's last swathe of freedom coincides with that of occupants. Piero Sartogo paints houses black and utilizes the Gescal towers as floors, undermining the repetitive space of the quarter. He raises questions about identity and facilitates the solution to the problem, something anyone living in a new neighborhood should do.

The use of color becomes a structural possibility, an alternative to three dimensions. It is defined in the complex reality of the mind, broadening the horizons of the real by organizing the interpretation of a system of relations of phenomena that goes beyond the objectivity of what has been created, i.e., the architectonic construction. The intention here, in one's perception of the object, is to raise the question of the quality of living, inducing the user to consider how to live space, when to live space is itself space.

Sartogo carried out the same operation in the Palazzo Taverna. In an architectural exhibition, he presented himself as an architect, but with an idiom that many architects do not know and do not expect. For Piero Sartogo did not plan his works in order "to exhibit them at the Inarch," as Zevi put it. Instead, he planned the Inarch show with the conviction that an architectural exhibit is not a composition of views and sections that justify one's work, but another creative operation, another composition of elements in which venturing into the labyrinths of the already done, the already completed, bears witness to the memory of the operator. And Sartogo composes the images of his architecture as examined mental space, as a possible and sacred linguistic channel, almost the only privileged factor in the architect/work and architect/user relationship.

The mental procedure is the same as that of every other occasion for planning, and the end purpose is also the same: to reassert a critical presence. Actually, the debate that it sparks is complex but accessible: A student of architecture taking part suddenly realizes that perception is the basic element "for future architects like us."

2

1–5. Five views of a design research project study model that explores "architecture as examined mental space, as a possible and sacred linguistic channel." Figure 3 is an aerial view of the model shown in the other figures.

But even this wrecking operation succeeded: It brought into the official club of Roman architectonic culture not so much a testimonial as a plan for a possible future encounter with a series of problems that could bring architecture back into artistic research: research that uses the imprints of the memory to create a historical position for the architect in his desire to find a common ground for discussion; a position in which the logic of utility is known, extolled, surmountable, and superseded; in which one seeks in architecture a "facies" that is at once its typological place, its typical user, and the architect's creative skill; in which there is no correspondence between iconography and society and the image is not used to undermine the present social structure. This kind of debate is no longer being conducted with two parameters — architecture as function, architecture as illusion — but with a third framework: space as dialectics, according to which the identity of space is its physical reality and its representation.

Here, one finds the great attention to the human component that makes it possible to communicate and to redeem the architect from the Oedipus complex he has about the modern movement. For that complex immobilizes contemporary culture in a sort of castration syndrome and in a conscience that is really fear of venturing beyond fixed assumptions.

Today, Italian architecture has discovered and is moving along the lines of participation, but it has not invented any idiom: Italian architecture has opened a dialogue with the masses, but with the presumption of having to use a more accessible language, a language of a lower extraction. But when baseness is in the planner's mind, what can one say? If it is true, as it was pointed out in the debate, that Picasso's work proved to be more accessible to the populist culture of the quarter than to the bourgeois culture of the Giulio Cesare secondary school, then Sartogo's operation is quite right in not seeking any such cover.

5

Without the presumption of talking another language, the channel of communications remains open not only for "authorized personnel" but also for those who live in the products made by that personnel. The completed work, the sign, and the image that redefines it open the discussion on what definition to give it and whether the definitions in our possession are of any value; and this may be a path to follow. In Sartogo, there is an interlacing of his awareness of a reductive reality, on the one hand, and a quest for reality, on the other: Amid memory, reality, and sign there is a perception of the question put by those who travel in the labyrinths of Borges, for it is in this conscious fable-myth-color and stabbing pain that the difference between architecture and building lies.

And building sends no messages and has nothing to propose. It exists, with all the mental confusion that it generates in its educational function of not existing and of supporting the weight of a structure of one cubic meter, as a model of happiness and non-thinking. It is with this kind of building that we have filled the territory, with the benevolent smile of covered space, in which no one explains how to live, for the simple reason that the right to live is itself denied, and the model home is the bad model of a culture exhausted by the certainty of not having the courage of reflection without analysis. And it is to respond to the one who, in the debate, stated that "the disappearance of architecture in the world must be accepted" that I say the appearance of routine building in the modern world must not be accepted.

This is a possible way, when the architect is no longer the technician of models — with all the historical distortions that, on closer examination, the most frequently used types bring with them — but the participant in a debate that struggles to express an idiom. Piero Sartogo and his virtual architecture are a moment of confrontation for a critical stance that has not yet been fully charted but can be; and it is not the only one. To accept the presence of two contradictory directions is the new historicist position, which cannot be explained with the presumption of a truth, but with the cognizance of multiform truths in which the subject is not the truth but the dynamic of truths.

The Rendering of the Void

Rome Apartment

1

RICHARD REID
The Architectural Review
October 1980

The apartment, even as transformed by Piero Sartogo is, in basic arrangement, a fairly orthodox free-flowing space. What is unusual about it is the arresting imagery that has been overlaid in the form of a series of implied planes that, in contradiction to the physical fabric of the apartment, create a totally new set of volumes and spaces superimposed one upon the other, creating a new kind of structure. These vertical planes, which cut across and divide the existing spaces, are implied by relief or incised planes of color and texture on wall, floor, and ceiling. The architect argues that there exists another dimension, an implied structure that lives in the voids created by the physical fabric, waiting to be articulated. As the open plan liberated the closed plan, this approach, in turn, yet further frees the open plan by rendering the walls as if they were part of the furniture or paintings.

The architect's brief for the ground-floor garden apartment in the 1920s masonry building was to redesign only the social areas, including entrance hall, living/dining, and bedroom/study areas. The existing fabric of the apartment was fragmented, leaving a large rectangular space with an area projecting to one side. Two freestanding parallel walls were all that were left to divide the main space. The entrance is on the inside angle of a rather bottom-heavy and largely shapeless plan. What remained of the fabric gave no indication as to what could or should be done to the apartment, except for the immediate constraints of entry. Any specific sense of imagery implied by the retained elements had gone, bar that of scale in terms of floor area (an additional bedroom and ancillary accommodation is tucked out of sight beyond the immediate area of concern). Any suggestion as to the zoning of the completed scheme was absent in the bared fabric. The apartment had been deliberately stripped of all but essential elements.

1. The Rome Apartment breaks the mold of conventional rooms. The new layout of space is achieved with vertical planes that cut through or across the existing walls.

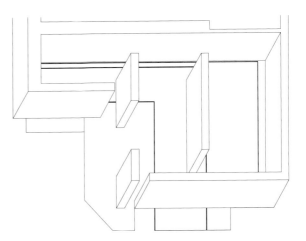

2. The apartment, reduced to the basic walling system, is L-shaped and subdivided by two freestanding walls. In the corner is the entrance area. Two balconies project from the apartment.

3–6. The first act was to lay down lines in the floor finish to define areas that are not coincident with the rooms as such. The lines cut through inside and outside walls.

4

5

6

No longer concerned with rooms in the conventional sense, Sartogo set about creating a whole set of "rooms" or spaces that on one level are illusory but which, for Sartogo, constitute the reality. His concern was not with the transformation of the spaces, as in an assemblage of objects, nor did he wish to leave the elements to themselves, as in the ready-made or found objects of the art world, but to re-create the idea of rooms or spaces. The project is based not on an explicit physical structure but on a conceptual one that is manifested by the ideal implied layout that transcends the anthropometric necessities.

Sartogo's first act was to impose a grid of angled areas marked on the floor plan, which partly follow, then cut through or across, the physical planes of the inside and outside walls.

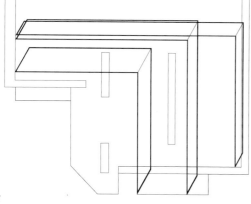

7

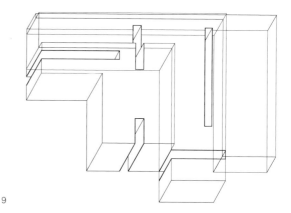

9

8

10

7–8. The next act was to transform the lines laid down on the floor into vertical planes via the articulations of walls and ceilings and the change of texture and materials.

9–10. The final act was to express morphologically the resulting three L-shaped volumes (fig. 9) as three spaces, each with its distinctive temperature and identity, the first being a so-called outside-inside with rusticated walls enclosed in glass blocks and typical sidewalk paving, all in gray (figs. 10, 15, 21), the second being an inside-outside with walls and ceiling in stucco and with terrazzo flooring, all in off-white (figs. 10, 20, 23), and the third being an inside-inside with wood walls and ceilings and carpeting, all in light brown (figs. 19, 22).

Secondly he reinforces the areas marked on the floor with vertical planes expressed by incised or relief surfaces articulating wall, floor, and ceiling. He thus creates a new set of volumes that, while they are only suggested perceptually, also have an eerie substantive quality.

Controlling these implied volumes is a series of perspective lines that transcend the orthogonal geometry and are generated from the entrance loggia. These perspective lines are articulated by light-colored bands inserted in the walls defining the main space and on the ceiling; they are picked up by an angled partition dividing master bedroom from study area and are reinforced at the generating point — the inside of the entrance door where door jamb and surrounds are built, or marked, in perspective. It is as if the room is enclosed in a cage of perspective lines, at times erased, so that you have the feeling of a partly eroded space of diagonals cutting across the orthogonally implied volumes and challenging you to shift your way of viewing the various spaces. On one level you have a delightful open plan, on another, a series of dog-leg spaces interrupted by freestanding walls, and on a third level, a series of apparently see-through rooms pinioned by perspective lines. To reinforce the implied spaces, the various volumes are differentiated by texture and polychrome bands taken across floor, wall, and ceiling. Articulating this further is a degree of inversion, as blind paneling is superimposed on key ends of the implied spaces, counterbalancing the real windows and occasionally cutting across the spaces, all the while introducing a surreal ambiguity.

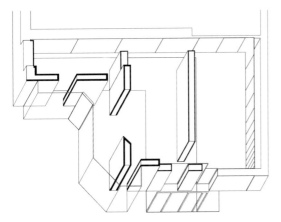

11

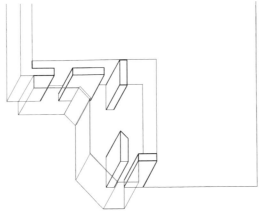

14

11–13. Synthesis showing difference in visual weight of rusticated, free-standing, and enclosed walls.

12

15

14–15. The outside-inside corresponds functionally to the entrance area in continuity with the garden and enclosed by the glass "almost a wall" block.

13

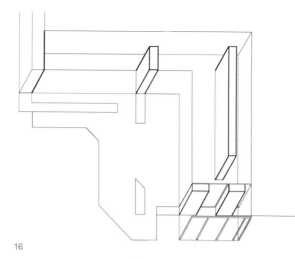

16

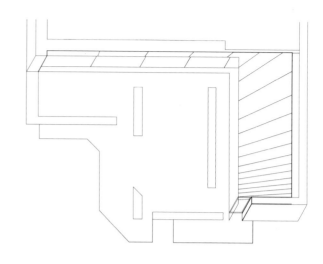

18

16–17. The inside-outside corresponds functionally to the living room–dining room area, which projects into the garden via the balcony (see also left side of fig. 13 and figs. 20, 23).

18–19. The inside-inside corresponds functionally to the bedroom-study, which also projects into the garden (see also fig. 22).

17

19

Finally, to reinforce the inside angle of the L-shaped volumes and to introduce a surreal ambiguity between inside and outside spaces, the angle itself is rendered in the manner of outdoors with the walls in the immediate area continuing the external rustication. The inside floors here mirror those of the external terraces, while the solid outside wall was abandoned for clear glass blocks that bring the light flooding in as well as transforming, from inside, the leafy garden outside into a kind of conservatory seen through a series of layers or frames, which Sartogo refers to as almost a wall. Most surreal is the way part of the glass-block wall can be swung inward, revealing a picture within a picture, a picture of rich jungle greenery framed by the diffused color of the glass-block surround. The effect of this secret window is of a glimpse into a world of Rousseauesque imagery heightened by its unexpectedness and the self-effacing manner in which it is done.

Having rendered the interior thus, one would imagine the client's freedoms to furnish it were at best severely restricted. Far from it. If anything, the strangely ambiguous "now you see it, now you don't" structure has generated an expansion of imagination that is memorable in its own right. On top of the physical and perceptual restructuring provided by Sartogo, the client has surreptitiously woven (to the architect's obvious delight) his own personal word of comfortableness that creates as lively a dialogue with the perceptual spaces as these do in turn with the physical.

However, the apartment project is not all it seems to be. The apartment, in fact, is really more a model for Sartogo's town-planning theories. Sartogo makes the point that before you begin to insert new structures within the existing urban fabric it is necessary to make an analysis of the component parts of the fabric.

20. View from the dining room toward wall facing the outside and its "window."

22. Bedroom-study view toward window facing the balcony and garden.

21. View of entry from living room. The door, seen from the inside, has the aspect of a front door as seen from the street.

23. View from dining room toward bedroom.

To understand the city, he argues, you do not have to analyze the whole city. Since the city is understood not through the buildings themselves so much as the spaces or areas the buildings mark, then the city image could be represented by only those key elements of the buildings that articulate the space or void between them. To illustrate his point in his project for the Nolli plan, he takes St. Peter's and suggests what those key elements might be. He isolates these elements, rather like a Gestalt completion picture, and then begins to transform them into another architectonic order. His use of St. Peter's is merely as an example to illustrate his thesis, rather than any serious suggestion to meddle with the cathedral.

Sartogo's concerns are with the articulation for renderings of the space (void) between buildings. To his architectural skills, Sartogo adds his considerable skills as a conceptual artist (both as painter and sculptor), for the designer of space needs to be that hybrid of all three arts.

For the city to accommodate change, it needs a coherent structure. The existing city, like medieval Rome, is generally composed of an accumulation of self-contained building complexes. As Ed Bacon pointed out in "Design of Cities," at the beginning of the baroque period the ordering principle chosen to guide the growth of the city of Rome was the establishment of lines of force that defined the tension between various landmarks in the old city. Interrelationship of these lines or routes and their interaction with the old structure set in play a series of design forces that became the dominating element in the architectural work along them. The cohesive element was a line of force, and the container for this line of force was the street picture, a central perspective in which everything of concern was framed.

Sartogo argues that the determinist frame of the Renaissance is unnecessarily restrictive and also that Colin Rowe's Collage City is too concerned with the last cycle in the dynamic of time — decay and eventual death — to be of use as an alternative. Sartogo acknowledges the need for the city to have an ordering structure, but he is suggesting a more subliminal and expedient kind of order.

He has recently developed his theories further in a study for the city of Bergamo. Analyzing the constituent plans of the city, such as the areas of collision between different formal systems, he began to isolate those key elements of the existing urban fabric that are sufficient to articulate the spaces between the buildings. Such elements might be a wall, or a molded string course or deep cornice, possibly a rusticated ground story, but together they can be connected in the mind's eye to form an image superimposed on that city or district. This exciting imagery can be further enhanced by laying grids over it that, in turn, suggest further possibilities for enrichment and extension in a wholly new order that cuts across, without destroying, the existing fabric. A characteristic of this proposed new order is a series of implied or superimposed walls or paths connecting existing landmarks with the new. The generating matrix in the Bergamo project is a series of volumetric envelopes, rotated around critical points in the existing fabric and used not to control the particular building height; the elements are those necessary to create the Gestalt completion picture of the city as a coherent structure. The walls of these building envelopes can be articulated in the manner of the Gescal Housing Development in Milan. Here Sartogo, in collaboration with Gianni Colombo and others, had planned a series of standard residential housing units in towers arranged quite freely, almost haphazardly. Planning was dictated by functional rather than aesthetic needs. The necessary coherence was provided by a light diagonal band drawn across the lower floors of the separate blocks, perceptually linking them, one to another, in the most expedient and economic manner.

In his essay "Aesthetic Appreciation of Nature," Ronald W. Hepburn points out that though by no means all art objects have frames or pedestals, many of them share a common character in being set apart from their environment in a distinctive way. In contrast, he sees natural objects as frameless. If one can accept the notion that the city is composed of both building and architecture, that one belongs to the vernacular, the other to the grand-design tradition, one a more natural (i.e., non-designed) object, the other an art (designed) object, then Hepburn's essay sheds some light on Sartogo's theories. Art is a language of symbolism, but here we are dealing with an art of an extraordinary dimension, including both vernacular and high art. In essence the city is composed of unframed ordinary objects, in contrast to the framed, esoteric, illusory, or virtual

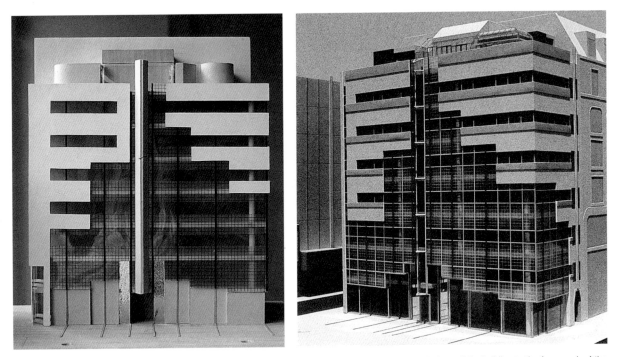

24. This project for a Geneva office building experiments with shaped lines to connect a public passage in front of the building to the framework of the structure itself.

character of the art object. There is a distinct advantage aesthetically here, although it does have its drawbacks, too. As Hepburn points out, whatever lies beyond the frame of an object cannot normally become part of the aesthetic experience relevant to it. A chance train whistle cannot be integrated into the music of a string quartet, since it would spoil the appreciation. But where there is no frame and where nature is our aesthetic object, a sound or visible intrusion beyond the original boundaries of our attention can challenge us to integrate it into our overall experience, to modify that experience, so as to accommodate it. Sartogo's urban theories are about the development of a frame that will help us integrate such illusions. There is no attempt to gate the apparently unassimilable, as so often is the case with the conservation area.

It is interesting that it should be in Italy, particularly Rome, that a theory that proposed a radical change in the means of analyzing the city, coupled with an imaginative method of rendering the void, one of Sartogo's key means of providing coherence in the city, should once again herald a changing concept of space. Even more interesting that it should be in a domestic project that such planning concepts should yet again first be realized.

An Artist by the Name of Gescal

Gescal Public Housing Development, Milan

2

Piero Sartogo's research into the expressive potential of architectural language, already displayed in his design of the exhibition "Contemporanea" and in the headquarters of the Medical Association in Rome, has taken an unexpected turn in the Gescal Public Housing Development at Sesto San Giovanni on the outskirts of Milan. A project of mixed adventures, full of provocative ideas, has been brought to its conclusion amid considerable conflict of opinion that resulted in the resignation of Vittorio Boracchia, Vito Latis, and Carlo Santi, who were part of the professional team.

BRUNO ZEVI
L'Espresso
October 10, 1976

The new housing complex is located in an area that is totally devoid of any town-planning. Five hundred apartments had to be constructed in groups of three 42-meter-high blocks, spread out along a central backbone conceived as a park area. Luigi Bugatti, Franco Casale, Grazia Michetti, Francesco Pagani, Sergio Rosso, Arturo Roversi, and Francesca and Piero Sartogo considered Piero Bottoni's town plan as an *objet trouvé,* assembling towers with painted segments in a grid pattern. Now that the work has been completed, the controversy has blown up again.

Sartogo defends himself: "There are some who discard this figurative experiment, accusing it of being 'super-graphic,' and others who can sense its structural message. To me the problem seems to be to understand what the distinctive limit is between real image and virtual image." He recalls relying on the intelligent assistance of the artist Gianni Colombo, expert in perceptive phenomenology. "Having established the vertical limit of the buildings and fixed the level of the secant plane that determines an above and below, we decided to tilt it in order to obtain a large-scale sign of identification and a hierarchy of proportional relationships to the nearby surroundings." The visual index of the process is offered by the yellow diaphragm wall, which extends as far as the pilotis on which the volumes stand, detached from the ground. The perspective aberration determines a sort of optical inversion, thanks to which the three-dimensional qualities of the buildings are annulled as "artificial"; they become mere surfaces, flattened shapes.

Also the roofs, painted like the walls, give the impression of abstract geometric axonometry. A "powerful" effect, devoid of sculptural indulgence, calculated to indicate the character of a fringe area full of heterogeneous elements: old rural buildings, the square with Bottoni's Town Hall, anonymous suburban constructions (built by speculators), factories, viaducts, electricity pylons, and smokestacks.

1–2. The Gescal Public Housing Development is at Sesto San Giovanni on the outskirts of Milan. An inclined plane intersects all the towers; the resulting segmented line of separation between upper and lower is a volumetric articulation reinforced by the separation of colors (white and black, fig. 2). Pedestrian paths leading from the parking lots into the houses are identified visually by the apparently disordered and fragmented system of the buildings' colored surfaces (fig. 1).

3. The scattered towers produce an image as if they were a united perspective. This design helps pedestrian to understand they are walking in the complex's central park.

The difference between real and virtual can be experienced by visiting the complex. At close quarters, we are surprised to discover that the blocks seem to be very spaced out. The "compression" that is evident from a distance vanishes almost like magic. Sartogo comments: "The overall picture that we have just memorized breaks up and recomposes itself in sections and sequences in relation to the pace at which you are traveling. Along the entry roads, designed as a network parallel to the towers, references to the internal courts of each housing group emerge. The courts appear as real shafts of air and color that intersect the secant plane, positioning the elements as if they were in a progressive numbered sequence. The pedestrian paths leading to the service areas in the district, instead, enjoy hyperbolic spatial dissolving views, inducing more of a mental than a physiological stimulus. We wanted to juxtapose the idea of space as information to the idea of anthropometrical space."

The immediate cultural references that come to mind are: the drawings of the futurist architect Mario Chiattone, the theory of "ugly and ordinary" proposed by Robert Venturi during the dying phase of pop art, Claes Oldenburg's colossal monuments, Victor Vasarely's kinetic contrivances, the objects constructed by Giacomo Balla. The architects claim, however, that "the way of illusion" has seeped into the modern scenario, generating "a schismatic movement that has never been transformed into dogma."

They cite Wright's Taliesin West "designed around a lane of nonexistent pilgrims"; the Villa Savoie by Le Corbusier, whose purist prism frames the "dynamics of the internal-landscape"; Richard Neutra's villas with their "air-conditioned" interiors and exteriors "that consume the panorama in a mimesis achieved through opulent glass envelopes." Sartogo continues: "Sooner or later, beside glorifying and glorified architecture, we will have to place more critical, liberating, demythologizing, and lively architectural examples. If in designing for reality we are traditionally and historically accustomed to 'see,' in designing for 'virtuality,' it is possible to 'invent.'"

4. The Gescal Development is composed of 27 towers of between 12 and 16 floors in height. The towers are grouped in threes around an open courtyard.

Subtle reasoning, bordering on paradox, which undoubtedly pushes one to experience the habitat not only physically but also psychologically. But it's a matter of compensatory devices, the fruit of unsatisfied space-time yearnings. Unable to transmit organic messages in Wright's footsteps, one is obliged to resort to the intellectual filters of optical art. This is understandable and praiseworthy in a crisis, but the risk is that the whole thing descends toward incommunicability, encouraging codes that are hypnotic, neutral, perhaps genial, but certainly devoid of humanity. Let's defend the Gescal housing development at Sesto San Giovanni, however: At least it stirs up discussion. It represents a protest, with desperate actions, and reasserts the right to creativity.

5. The proportional relationship of the black and white, which gives an individual identity to each tower, directs the resident to his apartment building.

Definition by Contrast

Medical Association Building, Rome

1

BRUNO ZEVI
Cronache di Architettura
1973

The first battle took place on the evening of May 18, 1966. The discussion regarding the projected building in Via Giovanni Battista De Rossi was becoming very drawn out when Piero Sartogo took some magazines and newspaper clippings out of his briefcase and spread them out on the huge mahogany table: "Gentlemen, here is the architectural solution for a Medical Association in a civilized country." The shock produced the desired effect: The building of the Royal College of Physicians, designed by Denys Lasdun in London's Regent's Park within an urban panorama, characterized by the subtle neoclassical tones of John Nash, appeared in the photographs to emanate extraordinary and irresistible charm.

Sartogo and his collaborators, Carlo Fegiz and Domenico Gimigliano, were then given a free hand.

However, a misunderstanding arose. The architects had no intention at all of drawing inspiration from the London building. Italian professional associations are not comparable with their British counterparts, and so the same project method, aimed at closely examining subject matter and programs to meet the client's needs, leads to completely different results. Here there ensued a second battle between the Lasdun building and the Sartogo approach:

"Marble floors in the offices and ceramic in the bathrooms?" "No, industrial rubber everywhere."

"Staircases with wooden steps or with fitted stair-carpets?" "Only metal."

"Plastered walls at least in the boardroom?" "Rough concrete as it comes out of the mold, and that's all."

"But why can't we have a minimum of charm, elegance, and refinement like our British colleagues?"

The architects were implacable: "For the simple reason that your Medical Association is not an ancient institution like the Royal College. It neither possesses a precious art gallery nor a series of extremely rare medical treatises. We lack a cultural tradition in the professions, and those seemingly odd but prestigious rituals that establish status do not exist. Furthermore, you have chosen a suburban location for your headquarters in a neighborhood full of apartment buildings: Do you want to erect a monument or a bogus Guild Hall? We will produce a significant work, you can be sure, but in a radically different sense from the prototype in Regent's Park."

This time the deadlock was overcome by Gabriele Crespi: "We cannot ask the 10,000 or so physicians in Rome and its province more than 500 lira a head as an additional annual contribution to supplement the modest budget we have at our disposal. The architects are right: no marble, fitted carpeting, and paneling; we must even do without air-conditioning."

Five years have gone by, but these events did not impede the construction of one of the most interesting and provocative buildings in the city of Rome, certainly the most original one ever planned for a professional association. Sartogo says: "Faced with a complex program, it would have been absurd to attempt a design strategy aimed at overall unity. Better to accept the problematic issues of the institution and the program, expressing them in the design with radical juxtapositions, one on top of the other. A discontinuous language? Yes, but the only valid one. We have followed the criterion of morphological contamination, manipulating both internal and external space in a poetic way."

1. The volumetric composition of the Medical Association Building in Rome reflects two major components: the very large public spaces (library, assembly hall, seminar rooms, etc.), directly accessible from street level, and the upper two floors, where the administrative headquarters are located. The lower part of the building is a concrete structure of large spans, while the upper part is a steel structure of small modulation.

2. The building, rooted like a tree, rises from the ground with a solid concrete trunk that is transformed into light steel glazed volumes.

3. The concrete elevator and the services tower meet the steel cantilevered volume over the vertical glazing of the stairway.

The configuration of the building springs from an accentuated morphological connotation of the different functions, juxtaposed in diachronic counterpoint. The virulent horizontal thrust of the metal parts and the marked cantilevers that offset the compact volume, already skillfully broken up by the architectural solution of the corners, counter the reinforced concrete structure, punctuated by distinctive vertical elements. Rather than using empty rhetoric, the language of the project selects specific and immediately comprehensible messages. Below ground level, we find the assembly hall with its annexes and at a still lower level, the archives, print shop, and garages. At street level, there are meeting zones and public spaces. Above this are located the periodical library and rooms for seminars, small meetings, and group activities. The top two floors are available for executive offices and the boardroom.

The principle of contamination is organically achieved. This is not an anonymous container with a regular structural framework into which rooms fit like drawers in a chest. The pilasters are coupled, and when required, they slide into a horizontal position expanding into beam-walls to envelop the auditorium, the cantilevered seminar rooms, the double-height foyers, and the periodical library. The result is an organism structurally engaged in modulating the interlocking continuity of the spaces and displaying their spatial volumes both inside and outside.

An analogous, coherent approach is found in its urban context. There is a sense of breaking off, a clear detachment from the apartment buildings of Via Giovanni Battista De Rossi and Via Antonio Bosio: The excavation has remained, the foundations are exposed to view, the building can be seen in its entirety, with its bridges and steps, like the roots of a tree, anchoring it to the soil. This exposure of the "roots" is the powerful, coherent result of the design strategy underlined above. The visual impact is thus of a grand scale revealing exceptional tension.

A tour de force, but in a positive and prolific sense. While the avant-garde loses vitality in its ideological masochism, the heritage of the modern movement is in the hands of young architects who tenaciously believe in architecture, in its problematic messages. A nonconventional list of functions, free from overwhelming syntactical expressions; a language that, by cutting out vernacular idioms and preconceived contextual historicism, falls into the mainstream of the modern movement in Europe.

In a few days, the third skirmish will be fought. A meeting of the association has been convened to discuss problems of interior design. Sartogo stipulates: "Another 800 lira a year is required to furnish it in the most basic and brutal way, coherent with the morphology of the space. We have already thought out every detail. No fancy desks, but trestle tables, metal shelves, and filing cabinets; Thonet chairs in place of Knoll or Miller upholstered furniture." Eight hundred lira: It is worth it to be able to complete a work that has been planned with the future in mind, a work of which Roman physicians will be proud.

5

ROBERT MAXWELL
The Architectural Review
July 1973

The primary impression is of an energetic and even violent display of gymnastics. The building is seen to be composed of independent volumes thrusting outward from a secret source of strength; at different heights these volumes balance above the surrounding garden according to the rules of an elaborate choreography — rules that are not apparent at first glance.

It is only when one has experienced the internal spaces that the principle of organization is realized. It turns upon the symmetrical stance of the two elevator banks. These straddle the lecture room, stand like sentinels at either end of the main concourse, and hold between them the kernel of the council room, high in the back of the building. Thus all the most important spaces are defined by their conjunction. This organizing principle is declared externally only through the symmetry of the upper floors, each of which projects a different amount on front and to the sides. In sum, an apparently picturesque conglomeration of parts dissimulates a resolute formality: Could this be an expression of the nature of the Medical Association itself?

The metaphor is not so far-fetched as one might suppose: Organizationally the work of the institution can be considered to be of two kinds. It offers to its members a series of facilities, ranging from the small library through the register of patients to the lecture and conference rooms: All these facilities are on display in the lower parts of the building, visible from the entrances and from the surrounding streets. But the institution also governs itself, and the administrative offices and council room, grouped around a secret garden, are withdrawn from display and placed high in the building to form a world apart. At the point of separation there intervenes a heavy double floor slab — a veritable shield — which permits the office floors with their small-scale steel structure to span over the more open spaces below. Private space, organized with severe formality, is thus segregated from public space, organized with no less severe informality.

In this deliberate ordering of the program into two distinctive realms we may see a search for definition by contrast. But the two characters of form thus combined in one building are complementary through their very qualities as differentiated form: The regular office floors cap the building, like a Florentine cornice, and contain the jumpy rhythms of the assorted volumes below.

Modern architecture has provided us with many examples of composition by differentiation. But in the prewar period the drive toward formal unity of expression was held back by a belief in the independent determination of each element by

4. The excavation remains exposed. The Medical Association Building emerges from below street level with the floating concrete volumes of the public spaces. From front to back, the three volumes are the print shop, the assembly hall, and the seminar rooms. The two-story void is the reception hall.
5. The concrete pilaster splits, producing a cantilevered wall to contain the volume of the assembly hall.

the program. Many of the designs produced for the League of Nations competition were of this sort. The most rationalist of these was undoubtedly Hannes Meyer's, in which the symbolic content of each part was denied: Each kind of space was accorded its "natural" expression, like being placed with like, and the whole defined as a loose association of elements, each of which was programmatically determined.

As the belief in the actual determination of elements by function declined, so did the acceptance of loose compositions. Postwar functionalism is marked by an insistence on the formal unity of each design, to an extent that segregates it effectively from its neighbors. In the typical brutalist building of the mid-1960s, the whole building stands out as a decorated entity, in which the differentiated spaces contribute as much as the differentiated materials. In the Boston City Hall, for example, the office floors are treated not as a distinct element requiring separate and uniform representation, but as a malleable element capable of being manipulated in the interest of the building as an entity. Boston follows La Tourette as much in the search for unity of form as in the simple imitation of its "high overhangs."

In Piero Sartogo's *palazzina,* the high overhang of the office floors provides a unity to the whole, creating a realm regular and withdrawn beneath which the more varied elements can be disposed in relative freedom and counterpoint. That the building belongs to the brutalist cannot be doubted: It is made clear by the limited range of materials and finishes, by the heating pipes displayed as guard rails in front of the windows, by the industrial steel staircase hung in the main foyer, by the imprint of timber boarding on the ubiquitous concrete surface — everywhere essential elements of construction are offered as a decoration to space, while space itself is offered as a decoration to the public realm.

Piero Sartogo has been fascinated by recent developments in the science of semiology, whereby the function of meaning has been extended from a word-based to a sign-based context. Words are signs used in a particular way — according to the set of rules we call language. Many other objects can be used as signs — but there does not seem to be a well-defined language of visual signs. Our ability to respond to visual objects as signs will depend both on the context in which they are used and the assumption that they are uttered as signs. Gestures are an obvious example of a non-linguistic sign. A brightly lit window in a dark wall could function as a sign in certain circumstances, whether exact or vague in intent. But such objects can only declare an intent in a very general way, and blue denims may equally signify today workman or trendy radical. The architect who tries to convey a set of meanings through the articulation of building form is usually concerned with a direct representation of function. But there is no one-to-one link between particular elements of form and particular elements of function, no lexicon of a visual vocabulary that would render precise meanings both simply and in combination. The most he can hope to do is to suggest a general relationship between building form and building function — a typology of functional forms. Alas this too has proved to be a chimera, as the variations of built form corresponding to a given function are virtually endless. Thus the architect who wants his building to exhibit an intention to convey meaning is driven to a kind of schizoid form. The building must be divided in character so that we notice a change of reference for each part. If we can create doubt as to whether the building is a simple entity, we simultaneously create a criterion by which the building can be judged to be a combination of signs. In this way it is possible for the architect at least to suggest the existence of a semantic "dimension." This is precisely what Sartogo has attempted in this case.

It is necessary first to achieve an evident consistency of the whole and then make within this a kind of contradiction. Sartogo calls this an element of "contamination." There must be some dislocation within the whole that will serve to question the self-contained completeness of the system. The break in character refers to the existence of a typology extending beyond the bounds of a particular work, and thus makes us aware of a semantic dimension.

In the Medical Association Building we can guess by their regular strip windows that the upper floors have a generalized function — administration — while the lower floors by their varied volumes and fenestration must serve a more particularized set of functions — social contact and publicity. One represents a private, the other a public realm. The parallel with Denys Lasdun's building for the Royal College of Physicians in London is obvious. That, too, reflects a division made by the architect

6. The stairway leads to the assembly hall, located on a lower level.

7. The building is connected to the street via a bridge.

6   7

in the program, in that case into categories of permanent and transient. In both cases the more private realm is clothed in a distinctive material and made to hover above the other elements in a gesture both protective and withdrawn. In both cases the visible change in character goes beyond the mere employment of a unifying superstratum — as in the Boston City Hall (1961) or archetypally as at La Tourette (1957). The assertion of unity is made against a divergence of character.

His intention is more explicit and more outrageous, for he has set out in the brutalist mode to extract the maximum of naked drama from his brief. All the elements are pressed into this drama. The site has been gouged out to basement level (for the car park) so that the building stretches up through six levels (emphasized by the staircase towers). It is a surprise to find that the building is not much deeper in plan, so heroic is the scale displayed on the main front, with its entrance bridge, moat, and projecting chambers. This is Rome, not London, and the light is an incitement. Another incitement, both physical and cerebral, may be found nearer at hand in that strange mixed-up building by the brothers Passarelli in Via Campania: Here no compromise has been allowed to temper the sheer confrontation of the smooth curtain-walled offices below with the jagged hillside of hanging gardens formed by the apartments above. This outrageous juxtaposition is greatly admired by Sartogo (he took me along to view it). The contradiction it offers is so complete, however, that its significance is in doubt. Is it two buildings in one, or two architects who can't agree? Does it genuinely extend the conventions of what can be taken together? Or is it doomed to remain a joke, like wearing a dinner jacket with jeans?

Something of this contradiction does come through, visually, in the Medical Association Building, but it is nothing like so blatant. It is a great pity that the civic authorities insisted on the upper floors being painted brown to subdue the gleam of bright metal that was intended. But the architect has also done something to disclaim the very "contamination" he sought by varying the projections of the two office floors. Through this variation they lose some of their distinctive typological definition. Particularly when viewed from the narrow side, the whole building merges together into a more or less picturesque composition of towers and cantilevers. If this means a gain in visual unity, it is at the expense of differentiation, and of the surprise and gratification it could offer.

I regret this, for the decision to break the building into two distinct parts seems to have been crucial in the architect's thought. Not only are the parts distinguished in external appearance, they are assigned different structural systems. And the built-in strength of that double floor membrane that separates them and supports the small-scale steel frame of the office floors must have been a costly item in itself. Costly also must have been the big-scale structural columns below, and the heavy concrete walls on which the meeting rooms are cantilevered at first-floor level at the expense of a useful flexibility within. The varied projections in the two office floors call for different office layouts to suit the different relation of column rows and window wall. While this may not in practice mean any great handicap, it suggests at the practical level that more attention is being given to the external silhouette than to the identity and rationality of the parts.

The building was commissioned in 1966, designed in 1968, completed in 1971, and is still neither fitted out nor occupied. Perhaps this is the Roman way, but it contrasts strangely with our home situation where new buildings are finished late and occupied prematurely. It appears that there have been changes in the committee responsible for commissioning the building, and the architect is confident that decisions of fitting out will be taken soon. But the story remains incomplete until we can assess whether the semantic dimension is reinforced by the pragmatic one.

ITALIAN EMBASSY, WASHINGTON, D.C.
Invited competition sponsored by the Italian Ministry
of Foreign Affairs, 1993, first prize
Client: Italian Ministry of Foreign Affairs
Status: Projected completion April 1998

Principal: Piero Sartogo
Design team: Piero Sartogo, Nathalie Grenon, Susanna Nobili
Project manager: Sergio Micheli
Architect and engineer of record: Leo A. Daly
Consultants: Howard Brandstone (lighting), Franco Zagari,
(landscape concept design)
Collaborators: Jairo Camelo, Roberto Lilli, Costanza Nobili,
Paolo Di Pasquale, Mike Lewitt, James Annovi, Claudio
Giudice, Arcograph

Further reading: L'Arca, June 1993; Architecture, Feb. 1994;
Architectural Record, Mar. 1994; Efeso, Mar. 1996; Casabella
602, June 1993

BANCA DI ROMA BUILDING, NEW YORK
New multistory headquarters building
Client: Banca di Roma USA
Status: Completed 1995

Principal: Piero Sartogo
Design team: Piero Sartogo, Susanna Nobili
Design adviser: Nathalie Grenon
Project manager: Sergio Micheli
Contract documentation administration: Soo Kim
Architects P.C.
Bank technical adviser: Vittorio Zoffoli
Consultants: James Ruderman (structural engineer),
Robert Derector Associates (mechanical engineer),
Howard Brandstone (lighting), Paolo Morselletto (stone)
Collaborators: Jairo Camelo, Roberto Lilli, Sebastiano Boni

CITY CIVIC CENTER, TAICHUNG, TAIWAN
International competition, 1995, honorable mention
Client: Taichung City Government, Taiwan, ROC

Principal: Piero Sartogo
Design team: Piero Sartogo, Nathalie Grenon,
Afra and Tobia Scarpa
Collaborators: Richard Reid, Sergio Micheli, Susanna Nobili,
Katia Alvarez, Claudio Giudice

BADIA A COLTIBUONO WINERY, TUSCANY, ITALY
Client: Tenuta di Coltibuono Srl
Status: Projected completion September 1997

Principal: Nathalie Grenon
Design team: Nathalie Grenon, Piero Sartogo
Consultants: Rodolfo Casini (structural engineer), Girolamo
Michelin and Maurizio Castelli (oenology), Carlo Stazzoni
(technological equipment), Claudio Marengh
(client technical adviser)
Collaborators: Sergio Micheli, Boudewijn Kaijser,
Claudio Giudice, Alberto Chiappini

MASTER PLAN OF DISTRICT BETWEEN STATION AND CITY CENTER, SIENA, ITALY
National urban design competition, 1994, first prize
Client: Municipality of Siena

Design principals: Piero Sartogo, Nathalie Grenon, Fabrizio
Mezzedimi, Roberto Burle Marx
Project team: Sergio Micheli, Luca Borgogni, Marco
Borgogni, Oriana Cipriani, Andrea Stipa
Consultants: Stefano Fabbri (civil engineer), Denis Creissels
(mechanical engineer), Richard Reid

Further reading: "Siena from the Station to the City" (exhibition
catalog, Alsaba), Apr. 1996

OPERA HOUSE, CARDIFF, WALES
International competition, United Kingdom, 1994
Client: Cardiff Bay Development Corporation

Principal: Nathalie Grenon
Design team: Nathalie Grenon, Piero Sartogo, Luciano
Damiani
Consultants: Ove Arup & Partners (engineering)
Collaborators: Richard Reid, Sergio Micheli, Gloria Arditi,
Claudio Giudice, Sebastiano Boni

ITALIAN PAVILION AT EXPO '92, SEVILLE, SPAIN
Client: Italian Ministry of Foreign Affairs
Status: Completed 1992

Principal: Piero Sartogo
Design team: Piero Sartogo, Susanna Nobili, Sergio Micheli
Film director: Michelangelo Antonioni
Consultants: Piero Castiglioni (lighting), Giorgio Caloisi
(structural engineer), Odino Artioli (media equipment),
Gino Parolini (systems engineer)
Collaborators: Giorgio Ducci, Jairo Camelo, Jan Strucla

Further reading: Ulisse 2000 no. 100, special
supplement (exhibition catalog, Electa)

NISSAN AUDITORIUM, CONFERENCE, AND EXHIBITION CENTER, ROME
Auditorium, conference and exhibition center, training
and offices facilities
Client: Nissan Italia Spa
Status: Completed 1993

Principal: Piero Sartogo
Design team: Piero Sartogo, Nathalie Grenon, Adriano
Caputo
Project manager: Roberto Lilli
Consultants: Mario Calzini (technology auditorium engineer),
Giorgio Caloisi (structural engineer), Maurizio Di Nardo
(mechanical engineer), Maurizio Baldieri (lighting),
Paolo Morselletto (stone)
Collaborators: Sergio Micheli, Fabrizio Lilli, Giorgio Ducci,
Jairo Camelo

Further reading: Giornale dello Spettacolo, Mar. 19, 1993

BULGARI STORE, NEW YORK

Showroom and headquarters
Client: Bulgari Corporation of America
Status: Completed 1989

Principal: Piero Sartogo
Design team: Piero Sartogo, Nathalie Grenon
Furniture design: Nathalie Grenon
Contract documentation administration: Soo Kim Architects P.C.
Consultants: Paolo Morselletto (stone), Howard Brandstone (lighting), W. A. Di Giacomo Associates (mechanical and electrical engineer)
Collaborators: Sergio Micheli, Massimiliano Leoncini, Frederick Biehle, Iwao Katumi, Massimo Magistri

Further reading: L'Arca, Apr. 1990 ; "730 Fifth Avenue, New York," L'Arca Edizioni (Milan, 1990)

INDUSTRIAL DESIGN

Glass Lamp, 1990
Manufacturer: Fontana Arte
Design: Nathalie Grenon

Tiffany & Co. Tableware
Client: Tiffany & Co.
Manufacturer: Riedel
Design: Nathalie Grenon, Piero Sartogo

Audi Chair, 1987
Manufacturer: Tagliabue
Design: Nathalie Grenon

Diamond Chair, 1993
Manufacturer: Poltrona Frau
Design: Nathalie Grenon, Piero Sartogo

Rondine Handle, 1990
Manufacturer: Forges
Design: Nathalie Grenon, Piero Sartogo

Ala Armchair, 1989
Manufacturer: Saporiti
Design: Nathalie Grenon, Piero Sartogo

BULGARI SHOWROOM AND OFFICE AT ZENITAKI BUILDING, TOKYO

Client: Bulgari Corporation
Status: Completed 1990

Principal: Piero Sartogo
Design team: Piero Sartogo, Nathalie Grenon
Furniture design: Nathalie Grenon
Contract documentation administration: Kazuo Adachi Architect & Engineers, Massimo Magistri
Collaborators: Sergio Micheli, Anne Sophie De Villepin, Iwao Katumi

Further reading: Shoten Kenichiku, Jan. 1992; Nikkei Architecture, Feb. 12, 1991; "Kekkai," L'Arca Edizioni (Milan, 1991)

ITALIAN PAVILION, TSUKUBA EXPO '85, JAPAN

Client: Italian Ministry of Foreign Affairs
Status: Completed 1985

Principal: Nathalie Grenon
Design team: Nathalie Grenon, Piero Sartogo
Scientific adviser: Giulio Macchi
Collaborators: Maria Vitale, Sergio Micheli, Iwao Katumi, Anne Sophie De Villepin

Further reading: L'Architettura, Mar. 1985; L'Espresso, Mar. 17, 1985; Exhibition Catalog, 1985; Scienza 2000, Mar. 1985; Il Tempo, Mar. 17, 1985

ITALIAN PAVILION AT CITÉ DE LA SCIENCE ET DE L' INDUSTRIE AT LA VILLETTE, PARIS

Italian Pavilion at the exhibition "Eureka l'Europe"
Clients: Italian Ministry of Foreign Affairs, ENEA (National Committee for Research and Development of Nuclear and Alternative Energies), CNR (National Council of Research)
Status: Completed 1987

Curators and design team: Piero Sartogo, Nathalie Grenon
Scientific advisers: Arnaldo Liberti, Vincenzo Damiani, Angelo Marino, Arturo Falaschi, Silvio Bevilacqua, Antonio Paoletti, Francesco Jovane, Claudio Battistoni, Lucio Bianco, Augusto Vighi, Fabio Pistella, Umberto Clemente
Consultants: Carlo Rosania and Patrizia Reviglio (audiovisual)
Coordination: Marino Marini, Ludovico Fulci, Michele Laddaga
Collaborators: Renato Balestra, Sergio Micheli, Patrick Gros, Olivier Glainzer, Frederick Cheix

Further reading: Exhibition Catalog, 1987; La Repubblica, June 11, 1987; Il Messaggero, June 11, 1987; Il Giornale, June 11, 1987

ITALIAN TRADE CENTER ON PARK AVENUE, NEW YORK

Multistory trade center and offices
Client: Italian Trade Commission, New York
Status: Completed in 1987

Principal: Piero Sartogo
Design team: Piero Sartogo, Nathalie Grenon
Client technical advisers: Roberto Lilli, Enrico Filippi
Collaborators: Sergio Micheli, Frederic Biehle, Larry Blumenthal, Gianni Rossetti

Further reading: Casa Vogue, June 1990

L'IMAGINAIRE SCIENTIFIQUE EXHIBITION AT CITÉ DE LA SCIENCE ET DE L' INDUSTRIE AT LA VILLETTE, PARIS

International scientific exhibition
Client: ISSA/AISA
Status: Completed 1986

Curators and design team: Piero Sartogo, Nathalie Grenon
Scientific committee: Paolo Budinich, Antonio Borsellino,
Roberto Pozzi, Edoardo Castelli, Ludovico Dalla Palma, Margherita Hack, Giorgio Sedmak
Scientific council: Stig Lundqvist, Benoit Mandelbrot, Tullio Regge, Carlo Rubbia, Abdus Slam, Dennis W. Sciama, Luca Cavalli Sforza

Further reading: L'Arca, Nov. 1986; "Memoria esposta," Italian Institute in Paris, Dec. 1986

1987 TELECOM EXHIBITION, GENEVA

Competition for the Italian pavilion at the International Telecommunications Fair, Geneva, first prize
Client: Italian Ministry of Postal and Telecommunications Services
Status: Completed 1987

Principal: Piero Sartogo
Design team: Piero Sartogo, Nathalie Grenon
Furniture design: Nathalie Grenon
Image coordination and graphic design: Nathalie Grenon
Consultants: Orfeo & Aurelio Giambanco (lighting), Antonio Michetti (structural engineering)
Collaborators: Sergio Micheli, Renato Balestra, Jan Strucla

Further reading: L'Architettura, Jan. 1988

TOSCANA RESTAURANT, NEW YORK

Client: Biticci Corporation
Status: Completed 1987

Principals and design team: Piero Sartogo, Nathalie Grenon
Furniture design: Nathalie Grenon, Piero Sartogo
Construction documents and supervision: Emery Roth & Sons
Consultants: Foscarini (Murano lighting), Vignelli Associates (graphics), Cosentini Associates (mechanical engineer)
Collaborators: Sergio Micheli, Robert Stern, Massimo Magistri, Roberto Gnozzi, Richard Blumenthal

Further reading: New York Times, Aug. 14, 1987; New York Magazine, Sept. 28, 1987; News, July 10, 1987; Lys Toli Flooring Trends, Sept. 1987; Restaurant Design (Whitney Library of Design), 1988

MASTER PLAN FOR FASHION INSTITUTE OF TECHNOLOGY CAMPUS, NEW YORK

Master plan for campus and design of new architectural configuration, 1983; Progressive Architecture award, 1984
Client: Fashion Institute of Technology, New York

Principal: Piero Sartogo
Design team: Piero Sartogo, Jon Michael Schwarting
Project architect: Jack Cain
Project manager: Andrea Clark Brown
Project team: Channing Redford, Kathleen Shea, George Schieferdecker, Tom Wittrock
Consultants: Edward and Kelcey (civil engineer), Paul Gugliotta (structural engineer), Bogen, Johnson, Lau, and Jeal (mechanical-electrical engineers)
Collaborators: Tom Brashares, David Griffin

Further reading: Progressive Architecture, Jan. 1983; Skyline, Mar. 1983; Perspecta 21, 1984; Parametro, June 1984

RENOVATION OF THE FIAT LINGOTTO FACTORY, TURIN, ITALY

International invited competition, 1983
Client: Fiat

Principal: Piero Sartogo
Design team: Piero Sartogo, Nathalie Grenon
Project adviser: Emanuela Recchi
Consultants: Gianfederico Micheletti (scientific research), Alex Fubini and Grazia Sartorio (urban planning), Vincenzo Ferro, Vittorio Silvestrini, and Pierluigi Bracciani (energy conservation)
Collaborators: Sergio Micheli, David Griffin, Massimo Magistri, Giampiero Bodino, Claudio Giudice

Further reading: L'Architettura 343, special issue, 1984; Exhibition Catalog (Fiat Group, Etas Libri, Milan, 1984); L'Espresso, May 20, 1984; Casabella 502, 1984; Domus, June 1984; Bauwelt 17, Apr.–May, 1984; Corriere della Sera, Dec. 17, 1983; La Repubblica, Dec. 17, 1983, May 21, 1984; Il Messaggero, Feb. 11, 1983, May 19, 1984; La Stampa, Feb. 11, 1983, May 19, 1984, May 20, 1984; Stampa Sera, May 21, 1984; L'Europeo, May 26, 1984

ITALIAN TRADE CENTER ON PARK AVENUE, NEW YORK

Multistory trade center and offices
Client: Italian Trade Commission Government, New York
Status: Completed 1980, redesigned 1987

Principal: Piero Sartogo
Design team: Piero Sartogo, Jon Michael Schwarting
Project manager: Edward Walsh
Contract documentation administration: Design Collaborative
Consultants: Vignelli Associates (graphics), Cosentini Associates (mechanical engineer), Irwin C. Cantor Associates (structural engineer), Gabriele Roos (color)
Collaborators: Peter Szilagyi, Giorgio Grosso, Arnold Rosemberg, Francis Halpern

Further reading: Architectural Review, Aug. 1981; New York Times, Sept. 17, 1981; Catalog ICE, 1981

ITALIAN RE-EVOLUTION: DESIGN IN ITALIAN SOCIETY IN THE EIGHTIES EXHIBITION

Touring exhibition of Italian design
Client: La Jolla Museum of Modern Art, San Diego, California
Status: Completed 1982. Exhibited at: La Jolla Museum of Modern Art, San Diego, Calif. (Sept. 10–Oct. 31, 1982); San Francisco Museum of Modern Art (Dec. 7, 1982–Jan, 30, 1983); Wadsworth Atheneum, Hartford, Conn. (Sept. 10–Oct. 30, 1983); Musée d'Art Contemporain, Montreal (Nov. 17, 1983–Jan. 8, 1984)

Curators and design team: Piero Sartogo, Nathalie Grenon
Advisory committee: Fabio Mauri, Giampaolo Fabbris, Alessandro Mendini, Bruno Zevi
Collaborators: Sergio Micheli, David Griffin, Joseph Kalman,

Carlo Evangelista
Research: Emanuela Bompiani, Umberto Silva, Stefano Casciani, Patrizia Pistagnesi
Coordination: Gianni Ratto

Further reading: Italian Re-evolution (Nava, Milan, 1982); San Diego Magazine, Aug. 1982; Los Angeles Times, Sept. 24, 1982; New York Times, Sept. 30, 1982; Los Angeles Herald, Oct. 11, 1982; L'Espresso, Oct. 31, 1982; Progressive Architecture, Dec. 1982; L'Architettura, Dec. 1982; Casa Vogue 137, 1983; L'Architettura, Jan. 1983; Domus 636, Feb. 1983; Skyline, Feb. 1983; Interni 328, 1983; Modo, Apr. 1983; Interior Design, May 1983; Epoca, May 6, 1983; Hartford Courant, Oct. 2, 1983; L'Espresso, Oct. 9, 1983; New York Times, Oct. 9, 1983; Vie des Arts, Sept.–Nov. 1983

BRUNELLESCHI ANTICLASSICO EXHIBITION, FLORENCE

Client: National Committee for the Fifth Centenary of the Birth of Filippo Brunelleschi
Status: Completed 1977. Exhibited at: Chiostri di Santa Maria Novella, Florence (Oct. 14, 1977–Jan. 31, 1978); Chapelle de la Sorbonne, Paris (Jan. 1–March 2, 1979); Chiostro Santa Maria della Pace, Rome (June 15–19, 1979)

Curators and design team: Piero Sartogo, Francesco Capolei
Scientific committee: Guglielmo De Angelis D'Ossat, Franco Borsi, Arnaldo Bruschi, Francesco Capolei, Mina Gregori, Eugenio Luporini, Pina Ragionieri, Piero Sanpaolesi, Piero Sartogo, Bruno Zevi, Ludovico Zorzi
Scientific advisers: Salvatore Di Pasquale, Piero Rosselli

Further reading: Cronache di Architettura 1181–1228 (Laterza, 1978); L'Architettura, catalog 1977; La Nazione, Oct. 16, 1977, Oct. 22, 1977; Finsider, Dec. 1977; L'Architettura 262–63, 1977; L'Architettura 274–75, 1978; Laboratorio, July–Sept. 1978

MASTER PLAN FOR NEW SCIENCE AND TECHNOLOGY PARK, TRIESTE, ITALY

National ideas competition, 1982, first prize
Client: Municipality of Trieste

Principal: Piero Sartogo
Design team: Piero Sartogo, Nathalie Grenon, Francesca Sartogo
Consultants: Ove Arup & Partners (structural engineer), Carlo Platone (infrastructure and systems), Giuseppe Gisotti (landscape)
Collaborators: Sergio Micheli, David Griffin, Antonella Amici, Giorgio Gugliormella

Further reading: L'Espresso, May 12, 1983; Il Nuovo Cantiere, June 1986

MASTER PLAN FOR CITY DISTRICT, BERGAMO, ITALY

Client: Municipality of Bergamo
Status: Design completed 1979

Principal: Piero Sartogo
Project team: Piero Sartogo, Luigi Bellini, Alfio Grifoni

Project manager: Cepro
Collaborators: Grazia Coppi, Franca Bettoni, Pippo Caprotti, Cesare Coerezza, Roberto Dell'Acqua Bellavitis, Vittorio Ingegnoli, Sergio Micheli, Guido Motta, Francesca Sartogo, Valeria Sborlino

Further reading: Cronache di Architettura 1229–1276 (Laterza, 1979); "Proposal for a detailed plan of the New City District of Bergamo" (exhibition catalog, 1980); Architectural Review, Oct. 1980; L'Architettura 4, 1981; Casabella, Mar. 1982

PARK AVENUE APARTMENT, NEW YORK
Client: Withheld
Status: Completed 1978

Principal: Piero Sartogo
Design team: Piero Sartogo, Jon Michael Schwarting
Consultants: Giulio Paolini, Joseph Kossuth
Collaborators: David Griffin, Tom Brasheres

Further reading: Progressive Architecture, May 1979; Architectural Digest, Apr. 1979; Soho News, Dec. 7, 1978; Gran Bazaar, Sept.–Oct. 1979; Process: Architecture 13, "Interior design planned space," 1980; Home Life, Feb. 24, 1980; Casa Vogue, Dec. 1981; Avenue, Jan. 1988

ROMA INTERROTTA CITY-PLANNING PROJECT AND EXHIBITION
Twelve urban-planning proposals based on Nolli's plan of Rome
Client: Incontri Internazionali d'Arte, Rome
Status: Completed 1978. Exhibited at: Mercati di Traiano, Rome (May 14–June 30, 1978); Congress UIA (Union of International Architects), Mexico City (Oct. 25–Nov. 31. 1978); Architectural Association, London (Mar. 14–30, 1978); International Fair, Colegio Oficial of Architects, Cultural Commission, Bilbao (April 12–14, 1979); Cooper-Hewitt Museum (Smithsonian Institution's National Museum of Design), New York (June 16–Aug. 12, 1979); Pennsylvania State University, School of Architecture (Aug. 27–Sept. 25, 1979); Italian Cultural Institute, Tokyo (Jan.–Mar. 6, 1980)

Design: Piero Sartogo
Consultant: Massimo Di Forti
Collaborators: Sergio Micheli, Massimo Magistri

Further reading: Roma Interrotta (Officina, 1978); Modo 13, 1978; Cronache di Architettura 1181–1228 (Laterza, 1978); Oppositions, Spring 1978; Architectural Review, 1978; Panorama, June 13, 1978; Controspazio, July–Aug. 1978; L'Architecture d'Aujourd'hui, Sept. 1978; Arquitectura 214, Sept.–Oct. 1978; Architectural Design 3–4, 1979; Progressive Architecture, Aug. 1979

ROME APARTMENT
Client: Withheld
Status: Completed 1980

Design: Piero Sartogo
Collaborators: Sergio Micheli, Giorgio Gugliormella

Further reading: Architectural Digest, May 1981; L. Vinca Masini, "Topology and Morphogenesis" (Biennale di Venezia, 1978); Architectural Digest, May 1980; Vogue, Sept. 1980; L'Architecture d'Aujourd'hui, Sept. 1980

GESCAL PUBLIC HOUSING DEVELOPMENT, MILAN
Low-income housing development for 2,000 inhabitants,
Client: Gescal Public Housing Corporation
Status: Completed 1972

Urban planning: Piero Sartogo
Image coordination: Piero Sartogo, Gianni Colombo
Design team: Piero Sartogo, Luigi Bugatti, Francesca Sartogo, Franco Casale, Grazia Michetti, Francesco Pagani, Sergio Rosso, Arturo Roversi, Luigi Visconti

Further reading: Casabella 380–81, 1973; Catalogo Contemporanea 1973; Bollettino Italiano, Diario della cultura e delle arti, Oct. 30, 1976; Piero Sartogo, "Immagine reale e virtuale," Centro Di Florence, 1977; Domus 579, 1978; L. Vinca Masini, "Utopia e crisi dell'antinatura, topologia, e morfogenesi" (Biennale di Venezia, 1978); "Cinquant'anni di architettura moderna italiana, 1928/78," Domus; "Assenza presenza, ipotesi su l'architettura," Nov. 1979 (exhibition catalog, Bologna); "Finalità dell'Architettura," Mar. 1979; Richard Reid, "The Book of Buildings: A Traveller's Guide," 1980; Anabasi, "Architettura/arte 1960/1980" (exhibition , Comune di Termoli, Dedalo, July–Sept. 1980); Drive in, Jan. 1982; Architectural Review, Oct. 1982

MEDICAL ASSOCIATION BUILDING, ROME
Client: Ordine dei Medici di Roma
Status: Completed 1973

Principal: Piero Sartogo
Design team: Piero Sartogo, Carlo Fegiz, Domenico Gimigliano
Consultants: Antonio Michetti (structural engineer)

Further reading: Domus 521, 1973; Cronache di Architettura 825–952, 1973; L'Architettura 209, 1973; Architectural Review 917, 1973; Casabella 380–81, 1973; "Cinquant'anni di architettura moderna italiana, 1928/78," Domus; Irene De Guttry, "Guida di Roma Moderna" (De Luca, 1978), p. 99; Richard Reid, "The Book of Buildings: A Traveller's Guide," 1980; L'Espresso, May 17, 1981; Spazi dell'Architettura Moderna (Einaudi Editori)

PHOTOGRAPH CREDITS
Pino Abbrescia: 128 (fig. 5), 129
Jaime Ardiles: 138 (fig. 1), 140–41
Claude Bestel: 94
Emmet Bright: 156, 171
Louis Checkman: 102, 103, 106, 107
Fontana Arte Photo Library: 72 (left), 73
Forges Photo Library: 78
Luigi Ghirri: 12, 66, 72 (right)
Jean Yves Gregoire: 93
Wolfgang Hoyt: 67
Andrea Jemolo: Cover, 16–19, 21, 22, 24, 25, 33–35, 37, 38, 40–41, 43, 45, 47 (fig. k), 48–53, 60–65, 76, 147 (fig. 2)
Minoru Karamatsu: 82–83
Norman McGrath: 26, 29, 30–31, 68–71, 86–91, 96–98, 115–23
Eugenio Monti: 126, 128 (figs. 3–4)
Ugo Mulas: 149 (fig. 9)
Matteo Piazza: 56, 57, 59, 80–81
Roberto Piersanti: 152–53
Poltrona Frau Photo Library: 77
Saporiti Photo Library: 79, 99–101
Piero Sartogo Photo Library: 8–11, 14, 27–28, 36, 39, 47 (fig. h), 56, 58, 84–85, 92, 95, 108, 111–13, 114, 124–25, 128, 131, 133, 135–36, 142, 146, 144, 145, 147 (figs. 3–4), 148, 149 (fig. 10), 150–51, 155, 157–59, 162–70, 173–181, 183
Edmund Stoecklein: 138 (figs. 2–4)
Tiffany Photo Library: 74–75

Biographies

Piero Sartogo and Nathalie Grenon are the principals of Piero Sartogo Architects, which has offices in Rome and New York.

Sartogo, born in 1934, received his undergraduate degree from the University of Rome in 1961. He began his career at the Architects Collaborative in Cambridge, Massachusetts, under the direction of Walter Gropius. In 1963 he received a grant from the National House of Japan and worked in Tokyo with Kenzo Tange and Kinori Kikutake. That same year, he established Piero Sartogo Architetti in Rome; in 1979 he founded the Design Collaborative in New York.

Sartogo received his Ph.D. from the University of Rome in 1971. He has taught at the University of Rome and is the author of numerous monographs on art and architecture. In addition, he has lectured at the University of Virginia, Cornell University, the University of Pennsylvania, the University of California at Los Angeles, Columbia University, and several European architectural schools. Sartogo is a member of the board of directors of the Italian Institute of Architecture and of the Italian Commission for UNESCO, a member of the scientific committee of L'Arca, and a former editor of Casabella.

Piero Sartogo and Nathalie Grenon started working together in the early 1980s with "Italian Re-Evolution: Design in Italian Society in the Eighties," a traveling exhibition displayed in major North American art museums.

Grenon, born in 1959, received her undergraduate degree in architecture from the Ecole d'Architecture et des Arts Visuels – Abbaye de la Cambre in Brussels and her master's degree in urban design from the Université de Montréal (with studies at the Harvard Graduate School of Design in Cambridge). She went on to two years of postgraduate studies at UNESCO's ICCROM center in Rome, on the restoration and conservation of historical centers, with a scholarship from the Italian Ministry of Foreign Affairs.

During these years, Grenon also worked as a set designer in Brussels, for both theater and cinema, and practiced urban planning and museum design at Blouin Blouin and Associates in Montreal. In the 1980s, she began lecturing on design in American and European museums and design schools and writing for L'Arca. In 1985 she won the national design competition for the Italian National Institute of Tourism's exhibition pavilion; the pavilion traveled to Germany, Switzerland, France, Belgium, and England.

Sartogo and Grenon's work has been shown in both joint and individual exhibitions at numerous museums in Italy and around the world: the Venice Biennale, the Cooper-Hewitt Museum and the Urban Center in New York, the American Institute of Architects in Washington, the Cultural Institute of Tokyo, the Palazzo delle Esposizioni in Rome, the Milan Triennale, and the Cayac in Buenos Aires.